Praise for Dancing with Monsters

"Amazing, a beautiful blending of honesty and creativity."

— Rev. Bebe Baldwin

"I laughed and I cried. You are an amazing writer—your book is a blessing because I have monsters that I dance with too. A wonderful inspiration!"

— Jennifer LaMotte

"I was looking for information and found inspiration...truly a gift."

— Paul DeAdder, Founder, Boomers Fitness, Inc.

"I wonder if only those with a chronic sickness in their lives truly know what it feels like day in and day out. I just gave up trying to tell others what it's like because I could never find the words. This story is the closest portrayal I've ever heard!"

— Ed Krawiecki, 15-year MS veteran

"I literally felt the book in my chest as I was reading it. It rang so true for me and my journey after the cancer diagnosis. Thank you for sharing so much of yourself so honestly, helpfully, inspirationally. You moved so effortlessly from your own experience to cultural expectations and reactions to an "intelligent observer" to a challenged traveler...which is just how it all is."

— Pat Nyman. cancer survivor

Dancing with Monsters

Dancing with Monsters:
CHRONIC ILLNESS as
CREATIVE TRANSFORMATION

2nd Edition

Kate Wolfe-Jenson

For Mom and Dad, Warren, Charles and Mary,
who gave me my first tools.
For the magnificent women of the Real Relentless Writers,
who move me forward through inspiration and example.
For Ralph and Alexis,
who keep me going each day with love and delight.

Table of Contents

Part One: Discovering the Dance

Monsters and Angels

The lights dimmed. People attending the art and spirituality conference stood in a circle at the edges of the university ballroom, facing the hundred feet of open space. One of the conference leaders , a dancer dressed in loose white pants and a white T-shirt, walked gracefully into the middle of the room. He was pushing a manual wheelchair in which sat Mark, a conference participant. I had eaten lunch with Mark the day before. He had told us of the diving accident that left him quadriplegic. As his assistant forked food to his mouth and raised his glass so he could reach the straw, he had spoken with animation about his job teaching college English. The leader and Mark began to dance. I don't remember music, though there may have been some. The able-bodied dancer pushed the wheelchair and let go of it, so Mark went gliding forward, fast, free, grinning. By the time he'd reached the other side of the space, the dancer was there to catch the chair. They moved apart and together. It was beautiful. It was graceful. It was holy. I left the room, sat out in the dark soft grass of the Carolina summer and wept. One of the conference staff followed me, checking to see if I was OK. "I have Multiple Sclerosis and there's a seventy-five percent chance I'll end up in a wheelchair," I sobbed. "They just taught me that I can be an artist no matter what."

I feared that illness and disability would rob me of creative activities that enriched my life: painting, writing and music. Instead, it turned out that while making art I developed skills I could use to come to terms with my life's challenges. What I learned about the creative process could help me deal with the frustrations of living with chronic illness (and life in general). If I could find creativity in the rhythms of overwhelm, surrender, accommodation and resolve that have been my experience of chronic illness, I could enter into a dance with illness and healing, rather than running from them. I could dance with my monsters.

This is a book about monsters. Not the cute, laughably incompetent ones you see in animated movies, but the ones you meet in your own life—ugly thoughts, unexpected losses, inexcusable evils. When I was a kid I thought that I was the only one with monsters. I never heard anyone else talking about them, so I thought I was alone. I disguised my monsters in piles of accomplishment and humor. I wrapped them in pretty words and colors. If I kept the monsters hidden, I thought I could fulfill my destiny as a young, Christian American. I planned to grow up and save the world...and get rich and famous and look good doing it!

This is a book about angels. Better than that: It's really a book about God. Despite my feeling that I was alone, God was with me and had, all along, been sending angels to minister to me. I didn't recognize them as angels when they arrived in my life, but I know them now. They are creativity, faith and compassion. They come with flocks of lesser angels riding their slipstreams.

The first monster I knew about was my monster-mind. I am not one of nature's optimists. I am, instead, an expert at negative thinking, catastrophizing, expecting disaster. I regularly descend into maudlin depths of self-pity. I wallow in muddy puddles of despair. I burst into floods of angry tears. As far as I know, I have had this moody disposition since before my parents rolled their eyes and pleaded with me to "stop being so dramatic." I thought that I would grow out of it. I didn't.

When I was twenty, another monster arrived: I was diagnosed with Multiple Sclerosis (a degenerative neurological disease known as MS). By then, I had a shelf of self-improvement books with titles like "Learned Optimism." I tried to be a hero, tried to look on the bright side. Within a month of the diagnosis, I vowed to fight the disease with everything I had. I took up jogging, a strict diet and meditation. I believed that with the right actions and attitude, I would beat the bad guy. I continued to fight for another ten years as my physical health and abilities slid slowly away.

My monster-mind couldn't have a better partner than the MS-monster. Together, they whipped me into a wild dance, MS tapping out fear, frustration and sadness and my monster-mind twirling it into depression, rage and grief. It seemed like the monsters were in control. The monsters would win.

But angels were already swarming to the rescue.

It was my exasperated, don't-be-so-dramatic, parents who pointed the way to two of my angels: creativity and faith. At the age of eight, I became a performing actress (a subtle rebellion), began the first of what became volumes of journals and started "making stuff". My monster-mind could work in my favor when it came to art. Big emotions and churning energy were allies providing the engine for creative expression. In those times when my monster-mind seemed merciless and unforgivable, I could turn to God. My parents taught me, by example and instruction, about a loving God. If God loved me, surely the hateful messages of my monster-mind must be lies. By the time the MS-monster entered my life, the angels of creativity and faith were already experienced defenders against darkness.

The angel of compassion has come to me in the form of support group members. By "support group," I mean a small group of people who gather and tell each other the truth about their lives in an atmosphere that discourages judgment and advice and encourages forgiveness and growth. The topic that brings people together doesn't much matter. The gift of the angel is that I understand that I am not alone. Others have felt the way I feel. Others have done what I have done, thought what I have thought and have found ways to live as if they are forgiven. There is nothing more freeing than confessing the worst and having another human keep looking into your eyes and holding your hand. Nothing can break down self-recrimination faster than the words, "Me too." In our determination to show each other our best, we deny each other those gifts. I have been blessed to be around honest, generous, unflinching companions who have helped guide me through the real world.

15

Putting up a good front for each other, we trick ourselves into thinking life should be easy; we separate ourselves from the wisdom carried by suffering and loss. We humans (especially we Americans) love progress. We like to see things getting better: stronger, faster, easier. We expect the same when it comes to our bodies. We also love to solve problems. Tell me what doesn't work and I'll try to fix it. Into such a mindset, a chronic illness—or even natural aging—lands with a thud. We've forgotten from whence we've come.

Not so long ago, we human beings were at the mercy of our environment. We were born, became injured and sick and aged and lived and died without understanding why. But curious, intelligent animals that we are, we started building and testing models with which to understand the world. We expanded our physical abilities by inventing machines to help us do our work. Thinking of our bodies as machines and using the new tool of scientific method, we started to discover cures for diseases and procedures to mend injuries. We began to dream of a world where every illness had a cure, where pain and infirmity were eliminated. But now, in the twenty-first century, new diseases and new variations on diseases are casting shadows over our dreams. Our old enemies are evolving as fast as we are and we find ourselves, still, at their mercy.

The trouble with our attachment to progress and problem solving, our romance with the story of triumph over adversity, is that it robs us of this moment of our lives. In this moment, I am strong and weak, fast and slow, ill and healthy, smooth and wrinkled. You are, too. Our heroes are always moving. They're riding into town, learning of an injustice, fighting the bad guys and winning, kissing the girl and riding off into the sunset. A hero without a quest makes a story without a dramatic arc. We love our heroes, our stories and our drama. But in real life, unlike heroic life, there is more being than doing. There is more slogging than riding. There is more diligence than drama. There is more playing than winning. We haven't given ourselves many models for our real lives.

I find myself wanting to play the hero. I want to tell you how to dodge the monsters, how to avoid them altogether. I want to inspire you in ways that will allow you to skip despair. I want the very act of writing to let me stand up and walk out the door without my wheelchair. But that's the dream world. What I have, right here and now, is my seated self, telling you about the ways I've found to be in this body in this world.

When I pretend I have no monsters, when I hide from them, or when I refuse to interact with them, I get stuck. My abilities to love and laugh and be a part of the world are impaired. Sometimes they shut down all together. My heart is closed. To get unstuck, I need to make what I stumblingly call an "internal gesture" and open my heart. By that phrase, I'm trying to explain some combination of deep breaths, mental emptiness and emotional tenderness that turns me toward life. When I choose life, I am released.

If I learn about my monsters…if I understand how they move…if I discover how to move with them…then we (monsters and angels and I) can turn this galumphing into a dance. It may not be graceful or polished, but, with it, I move toward God instead of running away.

In the essays that follow, I explore the landscape of chronic illness and describe its contours. Snippets of memoir, arranged in chronological order, tell you the outward circumstances of my life, while the essays are grouped to support my point: living with chronic illness is a creative process. I've included "creative experiments" to help you discover the landscape of your journey and learn about your own monsters and angels. My own creative experiments: art pieces mentioned in the memoir and more recent experiments can be viewed at www.dancingwithmonsters.com.

I wish that my journey had been more organized so that I could show you my beginning and end points and draw you a map noting scenic overlooks and washed-out roads. But that only works to chronicle heroic journeys and I am here dancing in hazardous terrain. I have noticed a pattern. I can lay the steps out in paper silhouettes on the floor. I can try to show you how it looks on different days, but when the music starts and the monsters and angels grab you by the hands, your dance may look nothing like mine.

Still, I invite you onto the dance floor.

Entering the Dance

The first contraction came when I was twenty. I saw it, simply and secretly, as punishment from God for grievous sins committed with a tumescent clergyman. It was a busy time. I was preparing for finals and an orchestra concert. My to-do list seemed endless. But I took the night off to go to a concert. Sitting in the darkness, in the red, plush seats of the university's concert hall, my legs kept twitching. The more I tried to hold them still, the more they seemed to jump around.

I was living in an old Victorian house with six other students. I walked home and told my housemates I wasn't feeling well and was going to bed. I lay in bed, shaking, feeling the darkness press close around me. There was no comfort in it. In the morning, when I awoke, I had extensor spasms in my legs. I didn't know to call them that, of course. I only knew that, getting dressed, I'd find myself standing on tiptoe without meaning to. Odd. Curious. Almost humorous. Not frightening— not then.

Later that day in class, my legs kept moving unexpectedly. I was paying no attention to the lecture. It was an urban studies class. I don't even remember what it was called. But I remember sitting three desks back in the second row from the door, feeling fear wash over me in strong and stronger waves. Then I did what I have never done before or since: I picked up my books and walked out in the middle of class. I walked the block home. I went into the living room, lay down on the rust-colored slipcovered sofa, pulled the zigzag striped comforter over me and shivered.

Over the next few days, the spasms and shivering stopped. But I noticed that my right ankle wasn't working. I couldn't always hold my foot perpendicular to my leg. A university health center doctor suggested that I had a potassium deficiency and should eat bananas. I ate bananas.

I gave it three weeks and then went to the hospital emergency room. The neurologist on duty was in a wheelchair. At best, he suggested, I might have a spinal infection that would take some months to cure. At worst, I might have Multiple Sclerosis, a progressive disease for which there was no cure. He wanted me to go into the hospital for a test, which would take a couple days. I called my parents to tell them what was happening and that I didn't need them to come. I called some teachers to explain my absence from class, got a ride to the hospital from a housemate and checked myself in.

I remember following the nurse down the long, dark, hospital corridor. I was being brave and independent. "I haven't been in a hospital since I was born," I said cheerfully, "so please tell me what to do." She left me in a room with a handout that described the spinal tap and myelogram I was to experience the next morning.

"This will explain it all," she said.

"A myelogram is an x-ray examination performed by a radiologist to enable your doctor to detect abnormalities of the spine, spinal cord, or surrounding structures," I read. It all sounded very routine and simple. I was terrified.

The next morning, I was given a relaxant and was taken to radiology. On a small monitor near the operating table, I could see an x-ray view of my spine. I could watch a needle being inserted. A small amount of spinal fluid was removed and some dye injected. The table was tilted up. The table was tilted down, "Catherine! Catherine!" They were calling me. I had fainted.

To recover from the myelogram, I needed to lie absolutely flat for twenty-four hours. My housemates visited, the most perceptive of them bringing with her my teddy bear. I greeted them with brittle cheerfulness. Mercifully, their stay was short.

When the nurse asked me to sit up the next day, I vomited violently and had a blazing headache. My recovery was not going well. My memory of events gets fuzzy. My parents came. The doctor delivered the Multiple Sclerosis diagnosis and started me on intravenous steroids. He discovered that my spinal column was still leaking fluid, which was causing the delay in recovery. My hometown boyfriend came to sit by my bed and hold my hand.

A week or so later, I was able to walk across the hospital room, picking up my foot and placing it normally. My eyes filled with tears. "That's pretty important, isn't it?" said my doctor from his wheelchair. When I closed my eyes at night, part of me seemed to be floating near the ceiling watching the self lying in my bed.

More than twenty-five years later, I live in brokenness and do not hope to return to all I once was. Most of what we hear about healing—from religions and cultures, practitioners and doctors—is wrong. It is not about getting back to where we were. Such a recovery is always temporary. From the moment I was born, I began aging toward death. So did you. From the moment I was born, I began to heal and so did you.

How shall I speak about a life pounded by the insistent rhythms of illness and disability?

Should I talk about the role of religion? The morning sun is slanting through a slender window, falling onto the low, round table and the squat blue candle that sits on it. The two of us are in the small office that smells of the candle and coffee. The door is closed. The painted saint gazes down with narrowed eyes as my spiritual director puts my young hand on his corduroy-covered erection saying, "When we talk about these things, all of me stands to attention." The diagnosis, when it comes a year later, seems unsurprising. How could God let such grievous sin go unpunished?

Should I talk about being one of the untouchables of American society? People alternate between staring and looking away. Physical therapists cheer me along for several weeks and then send me away because I'm not making progress. How wonderful it is when a child says,

"What's wrong with you? Why are you in that thing?" How stifling it is when a parent shushes and pulls the child away.

Should I talk about the tyranny of new age healers, who begin by suggesting that whatever they do will make me better until, after a few months and several hundred dollars, they begin to talk about making me more comfortable? Every time they look at me, their own failure looks back at them. How much easier it is to face the practitioners of Western medicine who talk plainly about the incurable and the baffling and tell me that, all things considered, I'm doing well.

Or maybe I should tell you how my heart broke the first time my daughter said, "I want a mommy who can walk." Or the sharp stab of pain, followed by a long slow burn in my chest when she said, "Come on, mommy, dance!"

My life is a dance and the rhythm is set by the drumbeat of chronic illness. There is the initial slam of physical loss, followed by echoes of grief and rage. I pull back, back, back into silence and protectiveness. Then there is a shift in direction. I cannot force it to come. I can only wait until I feel the change. I can use this moment of possibility to understand and redefine who I am in this new, diminished, body. I feel the swoosh of energy, move out again into life, until, BAM, the loss comes again. Illness beats in layers through my life: quiet, quick daily murmurs running under long, louder pulses. My work is always to allow the opening after the contraction. It is the work of giving birth to my self.

Healing is about throwing my heart open wide and taking it all in: sad middle-aged clergy who try to capture love with sex, well-meaning folks who see illness as something unclean, practitioners and doctors who ache to make it all better, children full of curiosity, children full of longing, dancers and twirlers and people who can't feed themselves. The miracle of being human is that we absorb what comes and use the fire of our hope and fear, revulsion and attraction, love and hate, to make a life from it.

I heard recently that a woman writing the story of her rape understood that she must first let her readers know that she was all right; she had come through to the other side. I thought: "I am not all right. I will never be all right." And, at the same time, I understand, deep down, that everything in my life is as it should be. "All right" is not about walking or feeling well. It is not about understanding it all or rising above it. All right is living in the muck, with legs that tremble, friends that leave and daughters who wish sometimes for other mothers. It is grieving the losses, accepting limitations and holding open space for miracles.

The Pattern of the Dance

I was in the shower, letting the warm water lure my body and mind into relaxation. As I stepped out, two pieces of my life fit together so neatly I can still hear the mental click.

I had been trying to figure out what to do for a master's thesis that I had already started to refer to as "The Damn Thesis." It felt like a piece of busywork tacked to the end of three years of what I hoped was scholarly inquiry into the psychology of the creative process. I had also been reading bunches of writing by people experiencing chronic illness. That morning, in the shower, I recognized the similarities in my areas of study: the journey of response to illness parallels the journey of the creative process.

In the short term, I was delighted to find a subject for "The Damn Thesis." In the long term, I had stumbled onto one of the organizing principles for the rest of my life. (There's an argument for higher education!) Shortly after I received my degree, I started presenting my ideas in talks before groups of people living with chronic illness and their caregivers. The sick folks thanked me for naming their experience. To my surprise, the "normal" folks told me I had described their lives, too. It turns out that living itself is a chronic, creative experience. I should have understood it earlier, but I was blinded by my youthful misperception that my suffering is unique and special.

Now that I'm solidly middle-aged, I understand that everybody suffers. Everybody has crummy things happen to them for which there is no cure and from which there is no recovery. Plans fail; ambitions fade; illness strikes; lovers leave; loved ones die. That's part of being alive.

It's one thing to remind myself that my struggle is a creative one. It's probably a conceit for me to suggest that the same is true for anybody else. I am driven by the need to find purpose in my experience, by the thought that these ideas are what I have to give you and I had better do it now while I can. So I give them. As my twelve-stepping friends say, "take what you like and leave the rest."

Overwhelm

My entry into a new cycle of experience with illness is always dark. It begins with hints of change. Physically, things are not quite what they used to be. Right now there is heaviness in the back of my head that (I know from experience) may evolve into a headache that will last two days. It is not yet two p.m. and my fingers are starting to fumble at the keyboard. I may not be able to finish writing this piece. My defenses leap into action. Part of my mind wraps itself around the idea of impending pain and disappointment. These subtle sensations can become so powerful that they cannot be ignored. I can't feel anything except pain or grief. I call this part of my experience "Overwhelm."

We might imagine that a creative process would begin in a sunshine-filled planning session, but that is not always the case. Scholars of creativity have labeled the early parts of the process "The Mess." We are called to a project, but the results of our efforts are unknowable. There is a sense that something is not right or is missing, but there is no clear plan of action. It is a bewildering time.

Too often, I fight against the feelings of Overwhelm. I keep on typing regardless of my fingers' response. I bluster to the next item on my to-do list. I try to ignore my grief and analyze the physical aspects of my situation. I try to control my surroundings and my body as much as possible. Perhaps if I ignore my emotions, they will go away. I always, sooner or later, lose this fight and give in.

Incubation

Sometimes, there is no choice but to be sick. I cannot keep working when the back of my skull feels like it's dripping down my chair. At some point, I will have to stop typing. I enter into a place of passive waiting and surrender. I need quiet and rest. Having experienced this surrender enough to know what follows, I have named it "Incubation."

In the creative process, too, we give up—temporarily—and do something else. We take a walk, work in the garden, take a shower, wash the dishes. While this may appear to be "time out" from the problem, it really isn't. Even though we're not consciously thinking about the project, we are continuing to work on it. We turn the project around in our minds for short periods and then tuck it out of our attention, but the problem solving continues. Formlessness and passivity are important qualities of this stage.

Reconciliation

For hours (sometimes days and, occasionally, weeks) I exist, dulled by pain or disability. I am simply surviving and waiting. Into this emptiness come flashes of life. The pain lifts for a few minutes or I am lifted out of it by a bird stopping outside my window, my child laughing, a momentary sensation in my right toe. The experience may be physical or it may be some kind of psychic internal shift. At such times, even in the midst of discomfort and weariness, there is a feeling that right now, in this moment, everything is all right and that, no matter what the future holds, everything will continue to be all right.

These moments of grace parallel the creative process called "illumination." This is the stage that gets the most attention in our culture. Because illumination is often described as the "aha!" or "eureka!" stage, it is easy to imagine it to be a joyous experience—and it sometimes is. Other times, though, it is a quieter "click" as the reasoning, judging parts of our minds figure out what is needed to make our imaginings become real.

These times, short-lived as they may be, give us precious seconds to remember all of who we are. They allow us to open ourselves to true healing.

Such moments draw us out of incubation and into reconciliation. Enough slivers of light enter into our darkness that we are willing to move back toward the day. We can't return, though, to what was. What we were is gone. Even if we expect to regain our earlier level of functioning, we have to integrate the experience of being ill into our lives. We have encountered the disorganization, the end, of what we were. We have been swept up in grief and frustration and suffering until we have no choice but to surrender to them. We have caught glimpses of a place of calm and grace. We are full of questions: What is happening to me? Who am I now? How can I live in this changed world?

We begin, slowly, to build relationship with our changed selves. We discover what is new about our abilities, our attitudes and our environment. We experiment to find out what works and what doesn't. We are not called upon, in this period of reconciliation, to make changes. Instead, we listen and witness what *is* in order to develop compassion for ourselves. We realize that we are enough as we are, even if we do not fit our old ideas of what is normal or healthy.

Rededication

As we become able to accept ourselves, we begin to open to our souls. We pay attention to what it is that we love. In the process of accepting ourselves, we may have sorted through many messages about who we should be, but aren't. As layers of cultural myth and social learning are stripped away, we reach the bedrock of our essential being.

We begin to express who we are. We begin to do what gives us joy. We take up long-deferred dreams. We return to the piano, start singing again, write, paint, study history, start support groups. In the chronicles of healing I have read, I see this pattern repeat. We rededicate ourselves to those things that are important to us. They are that much more precious because we understand, in a new way, how fragile they are, how easily lost.

The last stage of the creative process is elaboration and communication. We express our ideas in creative form in an attempt to communicate them to others. Any action can be creative, from making chicken soup to crafting a disarmament agreement.

Like creativity, healing is not a linear process but a cyclical one. Upon completing an historical review of theories of creativity (where the steps of creativity were variously quantified as two, three, four and seven) one scholar concluded that theorists were labeling the process rather than understanding it. So, too, I describe healing experiences without really understanding how they happen. For the purposes of a graduate thesis, it felt important that I find clear parallels between steps of creativity and stages of dealing with chronic illness. For the purpose of living my life, choosing to see the process as a creative one—with fluid steps and stages—is what's important.

Though I move through times of overwhelm, incubation, reconciliation and rededication, I do not move sequentially. Healing and creativity both double back on themselves, spiral down and skip. Creativity and healing dance, rather than march.

There seem to be smaller cycles within large cycles. During each flare-up (doctors and MS veterans call it an "exacerbation") of my illness, I return to disorganization, frustration, grief and the quiet of incubation. As I heal, I once again attend to my body, mind and soul and rededicate myself. These are the large rhythms of my chronic healing. Each day is different. A physical or emotional event may send me spiraling into grief or into joy for a few minutes or hours or days. These smaller rhythms nest inside the large ones.

Like all dances, healing and creativity require balance. I balance between doing and being, between stillness and movement. When I resist my experience, I clench myself around what has been, unwilling to make room for the unknown that is unfolding around me. I get stuck at that stage and feel powerless to take action. Only by opening to what *is* do I align myself with the healing process.

This does not imply that I should try not to resist. I *will* resist and *will* get stuck. Trying to control the process is just going to get me stuck in a different way. At their core, creativity and healing are both about release. With both creativity and healing, I need to let go and trust the process.

Diagnosis Response

My family gathers for Christmas. My eldest brother and his wife are with my parents and me. Another brother and sister live in other states. The turkey carcass has been carried to the kitchen. The table has been cleared, except for a few unused spoons. A fire burns in the fireplace. Classical music plays on the radio. My brother, a journalist, reads aloud highlights from brochures received from the MS Society. Knowledge is power in my family. We try to comfort ourselves by hugging it to us.

There wasn't much to know. My body's immune system was mistakenly attacking the insulating material of my nerves. As my nerves became covered with scar tissue, the signals would have more difficulty getting through. Symptoms could include blurred vision, loss of balance, poor coordination, slurred speech, tremors, numbness, extreme fatigue, problems with memory and concentration, paralysis and blindness. These problems could come on suddenly, might last for a short time and then disappear. Or, sometimes, the damage could be permanent. The intravenous steroids I received in the hospital were the best treatment of the time...to reduce the inflammation around the nerves and encourage the immune system to back off.

It never occurred to me to hide my diagnosis; I included the news in my Christmas card notes. I offered my boyfriend, Ralph, a no-fault escape from our relationship because I was no longer healthy. (I later discovered this is a common response, even among married people: "I will give you one chance to say you want out. If you don't take it, I will be able to comfort myself that I gave you that chance.") I tried to be brave and funny. I joked that I had gotten the diagnosis in honor of the International Year of the Disabled Person (which was just ending).

A classmate sent me Norman Cousin's book, *Anatomy of an Illness*. In the book, Cousins described how, having been diagnosed with a crippling and incurable disease, he (with the help of his doctor) took charge of his treatment. He checked out of the hospital and into a hotel. There, he watched funny movies (to help with pain control) and took large doses of vitamin C. He recovered completely. I wrote in my journal, "Cousins has answered a basic question for me. Do I fight the disease or give in to it? His answer is clear: fight like hell."

When I returned to school, I took each of my teachers aside and explained the uncertainty of my life under the New Rules. I was majoring in Human Services with minors in French and Psychology. Those areas of study value honesty and open expression of emotion, which made it easier to talk about impending changes. I thought I might be in and out of school because of MS exacerbations. I was hoping for the best, of course, but I wanted professors to be prepared for unexpected absences. In fact, I felt fine. My neurologist had said, before I left the hospital, that if I went without an exacerbation for six months, I would probably have a mild case of MS.

I had my second MS exacerbation on June sixth—six days short of six months after the diagnosis. I was dragging my right foot again and felt like my skin was being stuck with pins and needles. I was just starting the university summer session. For a couple weeks I went to classes in the morning and spent the afternoon and night in the hospital, getting my IV treatments. I walked with a cane. People stared. I had a gauze bandage around my arm, covering the IV plug. ("Football injury?" a stranger joked. "War wound," I replied.)

In the night, in my hospital bed, the fear monsters would gather around me. They would show me visions of my doomed life. I saw myself in a wheelchair at age thirty, unable to move, unable to go out. I saw my sweetie, condemned to a life of tending the lump I might become. It was my first experience of Overwhelm.

My favorite part of the day was physical therapy. Each day I saw progress. I was able to ride the stationary bike for a longer time. My balance was improving. My limbs were responding to my requests. My fear and pessimism faded. The fight seemed winnable.

A young man, also diagnosed with MS, was in physical therapy one day. Learning that I had a boyfriend, he warned me that the divorce rate among people with MS was astronomical. When he left, the therapist shook her head. "He gets better in the hospital and then he goes back to partying and not doing his exercises and six months later he's here again."

When the steroid course was complete, I was released from the hospital, fully able-bodied. The cane went into the back of the closet. I continued my physical therapy exercises at home. My boyfriend and I made plans to marry in a few months as soon as I graduated from college.

My sister-in-law sent me *The MS Diet Book*, by Roy L. Swank. Swank was a doctor who, in 1950, put 150 patients with MS on a low-fat diet (less than fifteen grams per day). Thirty years later when these same people were examined, those who kept to the regimen showed a significantly lower incidence in the progression of MS than those who deviated—even slightly—from it. A low-fat, vegetarian diet was a healthy choice anyway. I went on the diet.

I returned with diligence to a meditation routine. I had started practicing yoga and meditation in high school, then learned about and practiced Christian meditation during my earlier college years. I made sure to start each day with prayer and meditation.

Focusing on diet, exercise and meditation seems, on the surface, sensible and life enhancing. In some ways, it may have been both those things. Underneath, unfortunately, it was driven by fear. It was a subconscious bargaining session that was to last more than twenty years. "If I lead this healthy lifestyle," I was saying to the disease (to God?), "you will not disable me."

It was a unilateral deal.

Mac and His Monster

Once upon a time, there was a boy named Mac who liked to sing and draw and play baseball. He was also being followed by a large, gruesome monster.

It happened not suddenly, but slowly over time. First, Mac got the sensation that something was back there, but when he'd turn to look, there would be nothing to see. After a while, by looking very hard and squinching up his eyes, Mac did start to see a sort of heaviness in the air, like heat waves above hot pavement in the summertime. Slowly, bit-by-bit each day, the monster became visible.

It was huge, ten feet tall at least, with a sort of rhinoceros-like weightiness to it. It was a sickly greenish-purple color and its skin had the texture of rough tree bark covered with a thin shiny film of slime. As it breathed out behind him, Mac would first smell violets. Such a sweet smell would invite him to breathe deeply. Then a blast of foul stench would follow, full of decaying meat and stagnant water and unpaid bills. The monster said, "Hroo, hroo, hroo." It was horrible.

At first the monster simply followed Mac, shadowing his every move and breathing heavily on him. Strangely enough, no one else could see it, but they did notice that Mac seemed uneasy, blinking his eyes a lot and stammering.

Later, the monster became more bold. It coiled its rat-like tail around Mac's ribs, making it difficult to breathe. It poked him from behind with sharp claws. The stress was getting to Mac. He couldn't sleep. He didn't eat much. He spent all of his time worrying about what the monster would do next and whether the monster would ever go away and what hell his life would be like if it didn't.

One night, Mac decided he'd had enough. The next day, he began fighting back. He sprayed mace in the monster's face. He stabbed at it with knives. The monster roared with glee. The fight was on! As big as the monster was, they were well matched. They scratched and bit and sliced and hit. For all that day and half the night they kept fighting. Every time Mac felt a surge of strength, it seemed the monster did too. Every time he felt his energy fail him, the monster weakened as well. By midnight, they lay panting next to each other, exhausted, hurt and out of hope.

The next day, Mac wearily got to his feet. He dragged himself out the door. Right behind him was the monster, drooping over him with its hot breath, saying, "Hroo, hroo, hroo."

This went on for months. Mac hardly bothered to go out anymore. He and the monster stayed home, fighting each other one day, then moping around nursing their wounds for a week.

One day, Mac had to go out. He was walking down an alley, the monster slobbering along behind him saying, "Hroo, hroo, hroo."

"This monster is ruining my life!" thought Mac. Mac felt the anger come up in his chest as though he had a monster inside him. The beast behind him said, "Hroo, hroo, hroo." The monster inside Mac turned around and yelled, "Hroo, hroo, hroo!" And the monster shouted, "Hroo, hroo, hroo!" And Mac said, "Hroo, hroo, hroo!" They had a conversation, of sorts, there in the alley. Mac was pouring into it all his fear and anger and frustration and hurt. Sometimes they were loud and sometimes they were quieter and sometimes they hrooed at the same time and it was like...it was like they were singing together.

When Mac went home that night, he picked up a pencil and he started to draw. He drew the monster, over and over again. As he drew, he sang, "Hroo, hroo, hroo."

Things were a little different from then on. Mac and the monster still didn't go out much; Mac was too busy drawing. Because he was drawing the monster, he looked at it more. He discovered that sometimes it was bigger and sometimes it was smaller. Some days it was more purple and some days more green. Somehow, knowing that about the monster made it seem just a bit less fearsome. Mac and the monster sang to the pictures. They sang, "Hroo, hroo, hroo."

One day, there was a knock at the door. It was some of Mac's neighbors. "We were going out to dinner," they said, "and we heard music coming from your apartment. It made us think of you. Would you like to come with us?" Mac, who hadn't been out for a long while, went cautiously to dinner with his neighbors. Sure enough, the monster came along, saying, "Hroo, hroo, hroo."

While they were having dinner, Mac glanced back at the monster, who was still (by the way) truly hideous and looking at it almost made Mac lose his supper. But when Mac turned back to look at his friends, a strange thing happened: sitting behind each of his friends, Mac saw a monster. Some of them were large and some were smaller, some looked even more revolting than Mac's monster and some were almost cute.

35

When one of his friends said, "You know, that music you were singing back in your apartment was the most moving thing I've ever heard," Mac understood. He understood about fighting monsters and singing with them. He understood about having a monster and feeling different, but being so much the same. Mac looked back at his monster and smiled and the monster brought down one huge puce eyelid in a wink and said, "Hroo, hroo, hroo."[*]

---

[*] Visit www.dancingwithmonsters.com to order *Mac* as an illustrated storybook or hear audio of Kate telling the story.)

Creative Experiments in Discovering the Dance

Rules:

1. Use the materials and spaces of your choice: fancy or plain, special or ordinary, comfortable or challenging. It may help to pretend you're a little kid.

2. Do what you like (or change it so you *do* like it) and leave the rest.

3. Just once, try doing the one that seems most outside your comfort zone.

4. Be gentle with yourself.

5. Have fun.

Writing Starters:

Write the starter words and then keep going, keeping the words coming one after another even if you're writing "I don't know what to say next, but if I did...".

- The first monster I knew about was...

- My angels are...

- These ideas of monsters and angels don't work for me. It would be better...

- The God I know...

- Don't talk to me about God...

- It all started when...

- Should I talk about...?

- One pattern I've seen...

- Pattern? There is no pattern…
- If I would only…then…
- Healing, for me, is…
- Once upon a time…

Making your Mark:

With the mark-making utensils of your choice (color adds meaning and fun), make marks in response to the suggestion. Be as sketchy—or as elaborate—as you want to be.

- Make monster marks.
- Make angel marks.
- Make a map of your journey thus far.
- Make marks that show your dance.

Objects in Space:

Find a flat surface you can use for these experiments. You need to be able to leave it, have it be undisturbed, and come back to it the next day. Find household or run-of-the-mill objects or make your own.

- Choose an object to represent yourself and other objects to represent monsters and/or angels. How many will there be? What colors, sizes and shapes seem right? Position these objects in a way that reflects how things seem to be right now. Come back in a day or two and look at the space. How have things changed? Move the objects to reflect the change.

Sounding it Out:

Start with a rhythm—clap or tap on a surface. Add a repetitive sound—pitch, volume and duration are up to you. If you're a musician, feel free to use an instrument. If you're "not a musician," use your voice and body to make noise. Break free of the repetition and experiment.

- Sound like your monster(s).

- Sound like your angel(s).

- Sound like monsters interacting with angels.

- Sound like the beginning of your journey.

- Sound like an easy part of your journey.

- Sound like a difficult part of your journey.

So the Drama:

Set up two empty chairs, facing each other. As you change roles, move from one chair to the other. Feel free to get up and move around. If someone unexpected shows up, add a chair.

- One of your monsters is disagreeing with one of your angels about you and your situation.

Move Through it:

Make your body into a pose representing the idea: adjust your facial expression, how you hold your head and torso, how you position your arms and legs. Once you have the pose, begin to move out of it. Let how fast you move, how you move and how you're using the space grow from the idea.

- You start your journey happily enough, but run into difficulties. As you work to overcome them, you are beset by monsters and helped by angels. How does it end?

Part Two: Overwhelm

The Ways of Life and Death

Less than a year after my diagnosis, I am driving the thirty miles from my hometown to the apartment of my fiancé, Ralph. I am heading west on the highway, curving into an area known as "spaghetti junction." Traffic slows as two major routes cross and cars enter and exit the road. A muscle spasm pushes my right foot against the accelerator. I switch my foot to the brake pedal. More spasms give me only sporadic control of my foot. The whole event takes only seconds, but I am terrified. I tell no one. After I am married and move to "the Cities," I take the bus or ride with Ralph. I tell myself that not driving has nothing to do with MS. It is because we have one car and it is more environmentally responsible to take the bus. Riiiiiiiiight.

My first job after college was as an Activities Assistant at a nursing home. There were three residents with MS at the home.

One was a woman who was probably in her sixties. She spent her days watching TV from a reclined wheelchair that included padded arm and head rests. She had limited use of her arms but could speak and think. She suffered from osteoporosis (a common problem for those who spend time in wheelchairs) and told me she got compression fractures in her spine just sitting in her chair. I don't remember her name.

The other woman with MS, Lil, was one of the "stars" of the activity and occupational therapy departments. She couldn't move below the shoulders, but was very active from the neck up. "Transportation assistants" pushed her manual wheelchair to all the social and entertainment events at the nursing home. She used a mouth stick and a marker to make portrait and still life line drawings. She read voraciously.

Sid was the most able-bodied person with MS in the home. He could use his arms and one leg to propel his manual chair. I didn't get to know him very well because he died shortly after I started my job. MS-related swallowing difficulties caused him to choke to death.

Inside, I ran away from these examples of my worst fears. I reminded myself that MS is a very individualized disease. "Some people don't even know they have it," I told myself. I was determined that my illness would be mild. I continued to eat, meditate and exercise in ways that would (I hoped) produce a happy ending. I had no understanding of illness, aging or death and berated my job as "a cheerleader job." I worked at the nursing home for a year, distancing myself from my feelings, and then quit. I began working as a secretary.

Nearly five years after my diagnosis, I attended a facilitated support group sponsored by the MS Society for those "Newly Diagnosed and Mildly Affected." In the intervening time, I had experienced only one more exacerbation. My right ankle had stopped working again, my body buzzed with weakness and pins and needles. All symptoms had disappeared after a course of Prednisone, a corticosteroid taken as a pill.

I got a ride to group meetings with the member I admired most. She was a psychiatric nurse whose dependence on her cane had forced her to take time away from her job. Supervisors feared the cane could be used as a weapon by patients who were irrational. She and her husband had land in northern Minnesota where they were planting an apple orchard. Her descriptions of trying to plant apple trees with limited balance and mobility were comedy routines.

Another woman in the group made different choices. She was not visibly affected by her MS, but she had bouts with numbness and tingling and was having problems with incontinence. She complained about everything. She limited her activities because she was afraid she would tire herself. Her disease was the focus of her life.

The phrase that came to me was from the Affirmation of Faith I had grown up with in the United Church of Christ: God "calls the worlds into being, creates man in His own image and sets before him the ways of life and death." In the nursing home and in that first support group the ways of life and death were set before me. It wasn't the severity of symptoms that determined whether people with MS lived full and happy lives; each individual chose to open to growth and possibilities or close around loss and limitation.

I found comfort, during this time, reading and trying to practice Buddhism. I have never been a believer in One True Religion. In high school and college, I read about varieties of religious experiences thinking I would somehow blend all of them together in my life. I didn't consciously leave the Christian church, but I gradually stopped attending. I practiced "mindfulness meditation." Sitting cross-legged on the floor on the tan carpet in front of the sliding glass windows of the apartment, I would try to follow my breath.

I am breathing in. I am breathing out. I am breathing in. I am breathing out. I need to remember to buy pickles. I am breathing in. I am breathing out. My right leg twitches. Oh no! Maybe I'm going to have another exacerbation. And this time I won't get better. I won't be able to walk. I won't be able to work. I won't be able to do anything useful! Oops. I am breathing in. I am breathing out. Still, if I couldn't work, that might not be so bad. I don't like my job anyway. I didn't go to college to be a secretary. Sure, maybe it's for a non-profit agency and I'm contributing to the greater good, but this is not what I had in mind. And the bosses there are totally unreasonable. I shouldn't have to…oh. I am breathing in. I am breathing out. I am breathing in. I am breathing out.

Meditation was (and is) a helpful practice in the face of chronic, progressive illness. I was practicing returning my mind to the present, understanding that the visions of the future I could build in my mind in seconds weren't real. Dreams or nightmares, they were only electrochemical phantoms.

The Underworld of Overwhelm: The Demon of Depression, The Angel of Trust

Something in my body, something in my world, has changed. I am unable to make a motion I used to be able to make. What was once easy has become difficult. At best, I am disappointed. At worst, I am overflowing with grief and rage. It is hard to describe the experience of Overwhelm without rushing to explain how I emerge from it…how it all gets better. I don't want to stay stuck in the muck of grief, but that is exactly what happens. When I descend into the underworld, I am sure I will never escape it.

Here's my signal that I am overwhelmed by the challenge of living with chronic illness: I attempt some physical action, it doesn't go well and I begin sobbing. We bought a new bed, one that is, in many ways, easier for me. The old one was so high that, sitting on it, I felt in danger of sliding forward and tumbling onto the floor. The new one is low enough that I don't have that problem. Instead, I have a hard time getting up from it. After weeks of practice and problem solving, I developed an often-successful exit strategy, but at first it went like this:

I slide my walker into position, arrange my legs and feet so that they won't spasm and push down on the walker with my arms. My bottom lifts up off the bed, but only a few inches. Gravity pulls me back down. I know that, in this case, determination and stubbornness can be allies. I try again. Whump! Again, I'm back on the bed. Without thinking I say, out loud and with a teary whine in my voice, "I just can't DO this!"

There it is. At that point, klaxons and flashing lights should go off in front of me. Large orange letters saying "Caution: You are reaching

Overwhelm!" should appear in my line of vision. On second thought, that would just make me mad. Once I have reached Overwhelm, I am unreasonable.

What I need, at this point, is a day off or, at the very least, a rest. I need to sit with a paperback novel and lose myself in someone else's fantasy. I need to go beside a body of water and stare at it. One of the most irritating things about having a chronic illness is that I can't take a vacation from it. I bring it along wherever I go. Sometimes, even if I'm sitting very still, I can feel the thrum of the disease in my body. It's not that I don't forget, for moments, that I have MS. But it is, as they say, "in my face" every time I make a move.

Sometimes (increasingly often, I hope), I am smart enough to realize what's happening and take a break. Unfortunately, once I've reached unreasoning Overwhelm, I am too lost in my monster-mind to understand what's going on. I engage my determination, fueled by anger that I am ill and disabled and push on in ruthless disregard of everybody.

I am embarrassed to report that I have spent months, maybe years, in this state. This is why I squirm uncomfortably every time someone compliments me on how well I "handle" my disability. Like most people, I have some skill in displaying a civilized veneer even when I am, inside, a mass of writhing snakes and worms.

Overwhelm comes in so many varieties that it's possible for me to look and feel very different and still be lost in it. In addition to the flash frustration I've described, there is a very unattractive brittle anger I exhibit. Like the frustration, it's often the response to physical limitation, but the anger is directed at anyone unfortunate enough to offer to help. Someone once called it my "John Wayne act." I think I'm being gritty and independent. The person who has just been kind enough to offer to help thinks I'm an arrogant asshole.

The Minnesota State Council on Disability produces a publication called *A Question of Attitude* designed to help people feel less nervous when they are around somebody with a disability. Here's an excerpt:

You see a person with a disability who appears to be struggling to get a package off of the floor. You approach her and ask if she would like some assistance and proceed to help. She snaps angrily at you, saying that she can get it herself without your help. You conclude that:

a. you should not have helped her.

b. people who have a disability do not want help unless they ask for it.

c. you have just met a person with a disability in a bad mood.

d. all of the above.

The correct answer is c. and the pamphlet goes on to explain: "You cannot learn a set of rules 'for dealing with disabled people', follow them faithfully and expect never to offend. In this case, you just met someone who either does not like to be offered assistance or someone who happens to be in a bad mood for receiving assistance at that particular moment."

This is fine as long as my bad mood is not lasting several years.

Worst of all is the horrible sopping blanket of depression—my monster-mind at work. If I John-Wayne past all earlier warning signals, this is my destination. My particular brand of depression does not involve being unable to get out of bed. Instead, I continue my daily routine in a mist of grim, determined desperation. I know myself to be the biggest waste of space on the planet. I am horrible. I am nothing but a burden. The world would be a better place without me. Scrooge had it right: I should die now and "decrease the surplus population." I begin to make plans to kill myself.

It's hard to describe my dark thinking when I am not depressed, but since I have been a journal-writer, I have written about it when I am within the belly of the beast. Here's an excerpt, written when I was in my mid-thirties:

So tonight, when I woke from my restless sleep, the demons whispered: "You see? It's already here: you can't get a job; you're a burden on your family; you went too late to the financial advisor and if you go out on disability, you'll barely get any money. Your family's financial future is dark because of your presence in their lives."

And the tears start, because I believe the demons.

So here I am, exhausted and knowing I should be asleep and instead staring at a glowing computer monitor in the darkness.

What is the value of a human soul? Our culture doesn't know. We value people's actions...or scorn them. We value Stephen Hawking's mind, though we wouldn't if he hadn't become a success while he was able bodied. We value Christopher Reeve's courage, but if he had not been famous before his accident, we wouldn't know he existed.

Maybe that's my problem: I always wanted to be famous. Entertainers these days are internationally famous. Maybe the people around me value me for my mind or my courage. They just don't tell me. They're Minnesotans, after all.

This morning I threw away a plant that has been slowly dying in our bedroom. It's too dark in there, but we couldn't have it out where the baby could reach it. So I threw it out. I could have tried to nurture it back to health, but I didn't have the energy, so I threw it out. The work world has done the same to me. The difference is that I'm fully capable of doing good work; I know that to be true. Employers look at me and think, "Well, she might be OK, but she looks kind of sickly. I just don't have the energy to hire someone who will require special care." In these politically-correct times, they may not even allow the thought to be conscious. The other candidates for the job have a certain attractive something that I don't have. The employer may not be able to say what it is. I know: health. The Ivory Soap ads have told us for years: there's nothing more attractive than health.

So, here I am: thin, tired-looking, graying hair and in a wheelchair.

After enough descents on this path, I've begun to trust that my angels will save me. I don't take action. I move from suicide fantasies to escape fantasies. I imagine filling the van with gas, taking all the cash I can gather, going as far as I can go and disappearing from the lives of my loved ones, relieving them of the horrible burden I have become.

I haven't done that either. Maybe that means my depression is not true "major depression." It feels major when I'm in it. My angels tell me I have felt like this before and have lived through it, but, for a while, my monsters maintain my terrible orbit around thoughts of death and disappearance.

For the time being, the heavens are closed to me and I am stuck in hell. Though I claw the edges of my prison trying to escape, I always slide back down into the abyss. In saner moments, I may realize that ancient stories of descent to the underworld, rolling stones up hills or being swallowed by whales signal that I am not alone. But Overwhelm is not a sane time. It is an all-consuming plunge into pain and darkness from which I am sure there can be no escape.

Connections for a Good Life

Ralph and I are in our sporty red Mitsubishi Cordia, driving south across the gentle hills of western Wisconsin. I gaze out the passenger window, weeping. "I think I'm growing up," I sob. We have just said goodbye to my parents and are moving to North Carolina for Ralph's new job. It has been five years since the diagnosis. I live with a strange band of tightness around my lower ribs and background fear of an exacerbation, but I am able bodied and generally healthy.

Before we moved, I sensed that the transition would be difficult for me. It was to be my first big geographic change, the first time I would be far from my parents in an unfamiliar culture. I went to a drop-in counseling center. The counselor there was concerned about how distant I was from my emotions (This was a challenge to my perception of myself as a drama queen!). For several weeks I wore a rubber band on my wrist. The idea was that I "check in with my emotions" every time I noticed the rubber band and become consciously aware of what I was feeling. The counselor also suggested I "try to be more Italian" (She meant more demonstrative of my emotions.).

The transition of the move was exhilarating. There was the fun of being able to afford to rent a house, the beauty of North Carolina, the excitement of Ralph's new job. There was the pleasure of the earthy smell of cut tobacco that hung over Winston-Salem and the shock of seeing people with lit cigarettes in their mouths leaning over the produce case at the grocery store.

I was alone, unemployed and isolated. My driving phobia could no longer be hidden: bus service in Winston-Salem was not extensive. My mood plummeted and stayed low. I felt useless and hopeless. I started thinking about suicide, started considering its mechanics. During one tearful, late-night session, I begged Ralph to check me into a mental hospital. He suggested we try something less extreme first. I went to the phone book and found a listing for Emotions Anonymous.

As I was growing up, my family was blissfully free of emotional problems—as in "ignorance is bliss." People around us had addictions and difficulties and our job, as good Christians, was to feel compassion, supply hot dishes and give thanks that we had been spared. My mother had, on her religious reading shelf, a book by Jess Lair entitled, *Hey God, What Should I do Now?* In it, Lair described the changes he made to his life after he had two heart attacks at age thirty-five. One of those changes was to attend a twelve-step support group called Emotions Anonymous. I read the book as a teenager and recognized my reality in the first part of the first step: "I admitted that I was powerless over my emotions."

At seventeen, I didn't admit powerlessness. I was comforted by the idea that other people—even adults—had emotions so strong that they *felt* powerless. Part of being an adult was, I thought, having an intellectual understanding of emotions without feeling them strongly or giving in to their power. Had there been an EA group in my small town, I might have attended it. Instead, I listed the twelve steps in my journal, wrote a paragraph about each one and wondered why I wasn't happier now that I'd done them.

The handful of regulars who gathered in the upper room of a Methodist church each Tuesday night while I lived in Winston-Salem saved my life. They were the midwives to my rebirth. Laughing gently at my beginner's questions ("How long do the twelve steps take?"), they watched patiently as I wrestled with ideas of God. They answered "Me too" to my darkest confessions. Their love brought me—the real me, full of uncertainties and character defects—into the world.

In addition to EA, I began a yoga class. I doubt the other students knew there was anything "wrong" with me. I could do what my classmates could do. My only constant symptoms were the band of numbness across my ribs and tingling in my feet and legs.

Howard Kent, a noted British authority on yoga and health, came to Winston-Salem. He demonstrated his breathing technique with a young man with Cerebral Palsy. Before breathing with Kent's technique, the man walked a trembling three steps. Afterwards, he walked a more confident five steps. At the time, I found it an exciting validation of alternative medicine. Looking back on it, with more experience in both disability and "complementary therapies," I am struck by the human organism's ability to rise to the occasion. Mind and body work together to achieve peak performance, but such accomplishment cannot be sustained over long periods.

I discovered, with the help of my twelve-step friends, the connections that make life good for me. I need a few people with whom I can be ridiculously honest about all of who I am. I need to make pictures and arrange words into meaning. I need to hear music and be enfolded in the beauty of the natural world. I need to ponder and celebrate my experience. While I was in Winston-Salem (nestled in the beauty of the Blue Ridge Mountains), I returned to work, to art classes and to church. I discovered Creation Spirituality, which named and valued my creativity and mysticism as well as my urge to worship and my thirst for social justice.

At Christmastime, we visited Wisconsin and Minnesota. I felt my body relax into the familiar landscape around me. Ralph and I talked about how comfortable it felt to be there. On our return to North Carolina, Ralph began to look for a job "back home." By summer, he had found one.

Before we moved back to Minnesota, I attended a Creation Spirituality workshop. One of the highlights of my spiritual journey, it served as an open space to understand the transitions I was making. "Minnesota feels like home. I want to go home," I told myself. "Why am I so sad to be leaving a place I've only lived for a couple of years?" The answer came: "You were born in North Carolina." I know now that three important things happened in North Carolina that were the seeds of rebirth: I found a support group; I returned to making art; I returned to church. Seven years after squeezing myself tightly around the diagnosis of incurable progressive disease, I relaxed enough to begin to heal.

After the conference, I left North Carolina and drove, by myself, two thousand miles (one mile at a time) to join Ralph in Minnesota.

Dodging Grief: The Demon of Desolation, The Angel of Surrender

Sometimes the realization of physical loss sends me into Overwhelm. I feel as if the light begins to dim as the path descends. Other times a more subtle disappointment causes me to curl into a protective ball so quickly, I'm not aware that it is happening. I don't even know I've entered the dance.

In early 2003, I realized I had gone months without writing. Then, an impressive woman named Candy Pettiford spoke at my church. Candy is an actress who writes and performs dramatic presentations about the women of the Bible and about African American history. She becomes a dozen characters in the space of an hour. She sings in a voice that caresses you one minute and slaps you the next. She literally changes hats to change characters. As she does, you see her hands, made into claws by the ravages of Rheumatoid arthritis. She has had both knees and hips replaced. She is a powerful woman.

After her performance, I went to the bathroom to pee and discovered that, not for the first time, my hand was too floppy to use the catheter my neurologically-challenged bladder requires to empty. My daughter, Alexis, then five years old, was with me. "Mama needs to take some time to cry," I told her, simultaneously surprising myself and recognizing a truth.

I took December away from my writing project. December stretched to January and then March. "Why aren't I writing?" I asked myself over and over. I made up answers: "I'm too busy. My schedule is out of whack. Winter darkness is affecting me. I have writer's block." As soon as I said them to myself, I knew them to be excuses. I moved quickly to the next task, the next thought, to avoid the facts: It is a new year and I am in mourning.

I was diagnosed with MS on December 12, 1981. I was married on December 27, 1982. I was born on January 12, 1961. These significant dates are clustered around Christmas and New Years—all of them markers. Each date is an opportunity to look at where I am, where I was a year ago and what I've lost. I do not want to have lost. I rage over the losses, when I allow myself to feel them.

"I gave you my legs—don't you dare take my hands," I scream at the disease, as though it was open to negotiation. Believing disease is a demon might be easier. It would have a personality, a face, a pronounceable name. Instead, I rail against a brew of biological circumstances and their mercilessly impersonal progression.

We went to Hawaii for our Christmas holiday and twentieth wedding anniversary. It was in Hawaii that I first identified the difficulty catheterizing (though I'd been experiencing it for a couple months). Travel is not easy for me. Each time I take an airplane, I vow never to do it again. The airlines have it all figured out, in theory, but the reality is exhausting. For the trip to Hawaii, we "gate checked" my electric scooter so I could take it to the door of the plane. Because my walker would not fit in the airplane aisle, I clung to the seat backs as I walked to my seat. We try to sit near the front of the plane, but they often reassign us. On our return flight, I "gave up" and let the flight attendant help me to the restroom with the airline's "aisle wheelchair". It was so much easier for me that I promised myself I would use it next time—even to get to my seat. As always, I wage internal wars between my own and others' convenience.

Returned from Hawaii, I expected to write about surfers slithering through the curve of the waves, little children squatting next to Koi ponds. I wanted to tell delightful stories of tourists walking down the street with video cameras whirring in front of their eyes, of eating mahi-

mahi steaks beside a sunset beach, watching Polynesian dancers swaying in the gentle rain, wandering over Plumeria-carpeted tropical grass next to shining waterfalls. Those pieces of paradise *were* part of my vacation.

I wrote just such a paragraph. And then I stopped writing.

The next paragraph might have been about my struggles dealing with the not-very-accessible bathroom in the hotel where I often had to have help to stand up from the toilet. I might have described the exhausting transfers from scooter to rental car that climaxed with me looking down to see my foot in a pool of blood generated by a scrape my toes were too numb to feel. I might have whined about my exclusion from visiting the rotating restaurant in Waikiki or the historical sites of Hawaii because of stair step entrances. I was lucky enough to go to Hawaii. How can I feel anything but gratitude?

"Everyone loves a cheerful cripple," I wrote in my journal during my second exacerbation. "Well, sorry folks, but those cripples we see on TV are an illusion. The cheeriness is a thin veneer that has to wear off sometimes. There has to be someone to whom you can say, 'I'm terrified. I'm tired and I want to give up.' But there isn't. In the ten minutes it takes me to stand up in the mornings, I philosophize: 'One day at a time, one step at a time, somehow I'll make it through.' So far I have, but every day the steps seem higher and there are more times I wonder if I'll topple over."

The ancient Greeks told a story about Philoctetes. Pricked by a poisoned arrow, he whined continuously about his wound. His brave companions could not abide his complaints and stranded him on an island. That story reflects my fears: if I say too much about my real life, you will abandon me. Practicing to hide my grief from you, I become expert at hiding it from myself. It becomes a heavier and heavier weight until I finally remember to release it.

"About once a month," I told the members of a support group for people with chronic illness, "I have to fall apart completely. I have to cry and rage and whine." Looking around the room, I saw gleams in people's eyes. The idea of letting themselves go, of giving in to the burden of illness, was lustrously attractive. We so seldom give ourselves the permission. For those of us dealing with chronic conditions it is a psychic necessity.

Looking out the window of our twelfth story room in Kauai, my eyes traced paved routes toward the water. All ended in drifts of dry sand. "What good is a vacation by the sea if you can't reach the sea?" I pondered. Repulsed with the idea of being a spectator to life, I vowed to get to the ocean. I plotted a course with the least dry sand. At the end of the sidewalk, I revved my scooter into the dune. Ralph pushed the scooter from behind. Out onto the packed sand at the edge of the ocean, I could drive the scooter easily. When I stopped the motor, though, I could feel the scooter start to sink a bit. But I still had not touched the water. I bent over to put my fingers in it. My weight pushed one side of the scooter into the wet sand. The scooter tipped over and I with it. A wave came up and washed over both of us. I sat sideways in the sand laughing as saltwater filled my mouth. Tanning tourists ran to help Ralph get us upright and back onto pavement. Like a comic book villain, I was dry and clean on my left side, wet and sand-covered on the right. "Let's clean the scooter off here," Ralph suggested, brushing sand off the metal parts. He stripped the scooter carpet free of its Velcro fastenings and handed it to Alexis, then five years old. "Can you wash Mommy's carpet in the ocean?" he asked. She could. Knowing that the waves come in and out, Alexis threw the carpet into the ocean. We never saw it again. I picture it sunning itself on a beach in Fiji next to a glass with a paper parasol in it.

That adventure is one of the highlights of my vacation. It teaches me that engagement in life comes with risk. It reminds me that I have choices. Wisdom is found in experiencing sunset-washed beaches and bloody feet. Too often, caught by my ambition to be inspirational, clenched around my determination not to be a burden, I smile and move on. I dodge the grief. Denying myself permission to fully experience the costs of chronic illness, I find instead that I have refused its gifts.

Carpet Goes to Fiji

Once there was a bit of carpet. Perhaps it had dreams, as it was being woven, of gracing a fancy living room or warming small children by the fire. Instead, it found itself attached with Velcro to the floor of an electric scooter driven by a middle-aged woman with MS. There, it endured an almost constant bombardment of food particles, dog hair, paint and paper scraps. It had to go outside in the pounding rain and sub-zero temperatures. It was rarely vacuumed and was never washed. Sometimes it spent hours in unheated cargo compartments as the woman traveled by airplane. It was not an easy life, though the carpet consoled itself with the thought that it was doing an important service.

One day, after a particularly long ride in the belly of a plane, the carpet was trying to decide whether to be irritated by the sand that was being pushed into it or enjoy the warmth with which it was surrounded. Suddenly, it felt itself tipping sideways. A wash of warm salt water flowed over it. It had a sudden intuition that it was touching The Ocean—the wet blanket that enwrapped the earth and could take adventurous carpets to exotic ports of call. The carpet crinkled with excitement. For a disappointing moment, it felt itself moving out of the water and back to its usual horizontal state.

A moment later it was ripped from the security of its fastenings and was being moved through the open air.

It took advantage of the moment. It wriggled from the clutch of human hands and threw itself into the water it sensed beneath it. The going was rough at first but soon it was through the battering surf and out onto the swells of gentle waves, being rocked from side to side and carried into the unknown. Eventually, it washed up on the shores of a tropical island, where it sunned itself and gave inspirational lectures to beach towels under its new French stage name: Carpet Diem.

Identifiably Disabled

"And what does she want to eat?" the waitress asks, looking past me to Ralph. We are driving to Colorado Springs for a vacation and I am using a rented wheelchair because my MS has flared up just before we were due to leave. I am discovering the odd combination of being stared at one minute and counted as invisible the next that happens to someone with a visible disability. I am also experiencing the entertaining and frightening way my body responds to prednisone (a steroid sometimes prescribed to treat MS exacerbations). I'm waking each day at four or five in the morning, filled with creative, wonderful ideas. As we are traveling, I can only write them down, rather than act on them. None of them are dangerous, but they tend toward the grandiose. The meds are making me manic (Ralph could have used some of that manic energy as he pushed the wheelchair up and down paths in the Rocky Mountain Zoo!). Later, as the dosages taper off, I am filled with sadness and despair. When my neurologist tells me that steroids do not affect the long-term course of MS, but only shorten the length of an exacerbation, I decide I won't take them again.

In the late 1980s, Ralph and I worked full-time for Cray Research. I was still nominally a secretary but, since it was for the International Contracts department, I was able to work with people all over the world and translate contracts, which I enjoyed. It was the only time in my life I made mistakes that were known within hours on three continents.

Ralph traveled often and I was able to go with him to England for a week. With all the walking, I wished I'd brought my cane. When my legs got tired, they felt weak and rubbery. But we saw Stonehenge and Windsor Castle and stayed in a hotel built into the walls of Canterbury.

Walking was becoming increasingly difficult. I got a handicapped parking hangtag. I read the Americans with Disabilities Act's definition of disabled ("…a physical or mental impairment that substantially limits one or more major life activities") and, for the first time, counted myself in. Walking longer distances, even with a cane, was getting more difficult. With the help of my doctor and the insurance company, I purchased an electric scooter, which I used very occasionally.

Unfortunately, the scooter was heavy. Lifting the disassembled pieces from the trunk of the car and assembling them left me exhausted (as did reversing the process).

One embarrassing symptom that developed while I was at Cray was bladder incontinence. I couldn't make it to the bathroom fast enough, so I started wearing pads in my underwear all the time. The urologist said, "I'm going to give you back your life," and I understood what he meant. With the medication he prescribed, I did not have to locate and use the bathroom in each building I visited.

I enjoyed my job at Cray (and, though I didn't know it, I was at the height of my earning power) but I wasn't satisfied with my ethical contribution to the world. I began doing crisis phone counseling one night a week at a local non-profit agency. Those nights convinced me that I wanted a career change. I entered graduate school to study psychology. I enjoyed school, but I was uncomfortable with what felt to me to be narrow views of what counted as "healthy" human behavior and limited tools with which to empower people. I switched to a Human Development major, thinking I would become an art therapist.

My job at Cray ended when I complained that, though I was translating and abstracting contracts, I was getting paid as a secretary. The Human Resources department advised me to stop translating contracts. I resigned in a snit.

A few months later, the drop-foot symptom returned and didn't go away. I used the cane all the time and was fitted for a plastic brace that kept my ankle at a right angle so I could walk more easily. We bought a manual wheelchair. It was more work than the scooter to use once I was in it, but at least it was easier to transport.

I got a job as a part-time counselor at a drop-in center for people with "serious and persistent mental illness." Among other things, I offered art activities to the people who used the center. Those who deal with mental illness are experts in living with chronic illness. Mental illness often becomes evident as someone reaches early adulthood and can be devastating in its effects on a life. It's often difficult to find and keep employment, the stigma is enormous and the collateral damage done by psychotropic medications is dreadful. The people around me at the drop-in center taught me, by example, about compassion, perseverance and courage.

They also taught me that I did not want to be an art therapist. Launching myself into the unknown (the blank page), inviting metaphors to show me new things, integrating unexpected movements so they become part of the whole instead of mistakes—these are the tasks of art and I love them. Some people find these activities frightening; some find them useless. When I tried to make art important and meaningful for people who were not interested, I felt frustrated and a failure. When I was selfish with my art, making it just for my own pleasure, it fed my soul.

Creative Experiments in Overwhelm

Rules Review:

1. Use the materials and spaces of your choice: fancy or plain, special or ordinary, comfortable or challenging. It may help to pretend you're a little kid.

2. Do what you like (or change it so you *do* like it) and leave the rest.

3. Just once, try doing the one that seems most outside your comfort zone.

4. Be gentle with yourself.

5. Have fun.

Writing Starters:

Write the starter words and then keep going, keeping the words coming one after another even if you're writing "I don't know what to say next, but if I did...".

- One of my toughest times was...

- When it gets to be too much, I...

- My favorite moments are...

- A signal that I am overwhelmed is...

- What I need when I am overwhelmed is...

- I don't really get overwhelmed. Instead...

- I am powerless over…

- What nourishes me most is…I can't surrender because…

- The ingredients of a good life are…

- Healing, for me, is…

- Once upon a time…

Making your Mark:

With the mark-making utensils of your choice (color adds meaning and fun), make marks in response to the suggestion. Be as sketchy—or as elaborate—as you want to be.

- Make bad, evil, horrible marks.

- Make one mark that represents you. Overwhelm it with other marks.

- Make marks that represent your biggest challenge.

- Make surrendering, trusting marks.

Objects in Space:

Find a flat surface you can use for these experiments. You need to be able to leave it, have it be undisturbed, and come back to it the next day. Find household or run-of-the-mill objects or make your own.

- Choose an object to represent you. Choose other objects that represent challenges you face, things demanding your attention, uncomfortable situations. Overwhelm the "you" object with the others. Come back in a day or two and look at the space. If you feel an urge to rescue yourself, resist for a few minutes.

Sounding it Out:

Start with a rhythm—clap or tap on a surface. Add a repetitive sound—pitch, volume and duration are up to you. If you're a musician, feel free to use an instrument. If you're "not a musician," use your voice and body to make noise. Break free of the repetition and experiment.

- Sound like relaxation.

- Sound like expanding fear.

- Sound like repeating anger.

- Combine fear and anger and then try to smother them; Sound like depression.

- Sound like surrender.

- Sound like trust.

So the Drama:

Set up two empty chairs, facing each other. As you change roles, move from one chair to the other. Feel free to get up and move around. If someone unexpected shows up, add a chair.

- Your overwhelmed self is whining to a relentlessly upbeat or heroic self about how things have changed.

Move Through it:

Make your body into a pose representing the idea: adjust your facial expression, how you hold your head and torso, how you position your arms and legs. Once you have the pose, begin to move out of it. Let how fast you move, how you move and how you're using the space grow from the idea.

- You are moving along normally. You encounter a heavy load. (Does it fall on you? Do you bump into it?) It overwhelms you to the point that you stop moving.

Part Three: Incubation

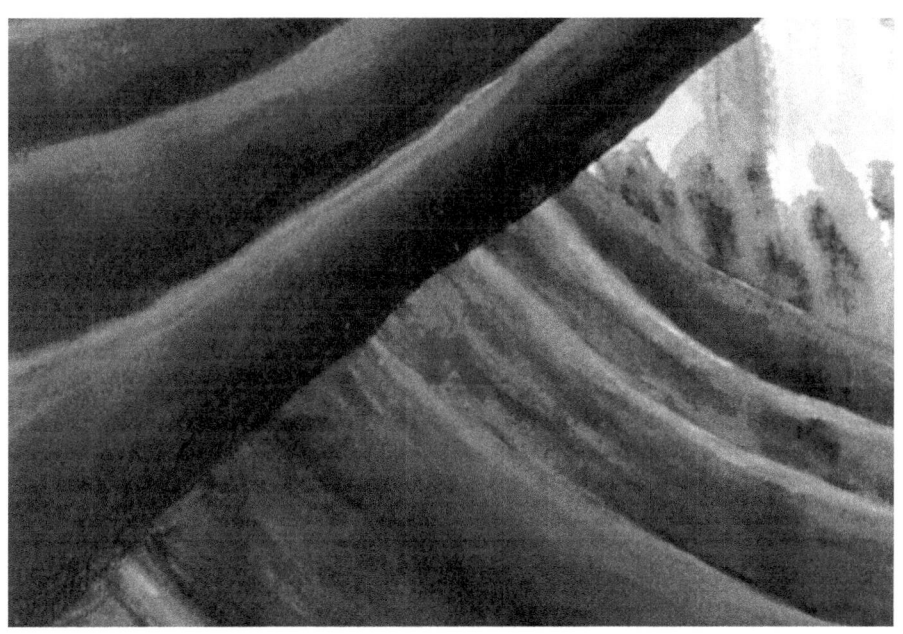

An Unexpected Turn

Sally Brown quietly considers the pastel drawings scattered across the wooden studio floor. I have begun to suspect that my plan to be an art therapist is a "projection." Encouraging people at the drop-in center to do art seems to frustrate all of us. They are more comfortable with craft projects. I want *them* to make art because *I* want to make art. Sally points to a drawing I've done called "Bodygrief," a self-portrait of a naked me in a fetal position. "Of course your illness will be part of your art," she says. I am flooded with relief. "A part" of my art, she has said, not all of it. I am more than my disease. I begin studying painting with Sally, spending one morning a week with a handful of women in her sunny studio, indulging in art making. I love it.

Thirteen years after diagnosis, I earned my master's degree in Human Development. My thesis was the seed for this book: *Chronic Illness as Creative Transformation*, a scholarly comparison of theories of creativity and accounts of chronic physical and mental illness. The university required me to present my ideas at a public forum. I hung my paintings on the walls, told the story of "Mac and his Monster," and talked about the connections between the creative process and living with chronic illness. I did several similar presentations for community groups and classes. It felt right. It felt like I was fulfilling a Purpose. Then life intervened.

While I was working at the drop-in center, we were part of an effort to "get technology to the technology have-nots." In preparation for that undertaking, I learned how to make Internet Web pages.

When the county cut the agency's budget and "defunded" my position, I decided to open a business teaching people to make their own Web pages. My thought was that this would be a "side business" that would support my art and writing habits. My timing was perfect; Web use would quadruple in the next three years.

Soon, I was designing and building Web pages for clients, mostly non-profit or governmental organizations. Within three years, I had a business partner who did programming and the business had two employees. Ralph had his own business as an Internet access provider and we both worked most of our waking hours. I loved the challenge, creativity and (I admit) the cachet of being an entrepreneur.

About this time, I started having symptoms in my hands. Later in the day, my fingers would get clumsy. They were numb and tingly most of the time. This was terrifyingly similar to the early symptoms in my legs. It was easy (though not helpful) to imagine that in ten years I might not be able to use my hands.

Ten years previously, we had decided we were ready to have children. I stopped using birth control. When I didn't conceive, we discussed taking more extreme action, but decided fertility treatments didn't make sense for us. I read that human bodies were smart enough to know if they were too ill to have a child. After a few years of increasing disability, I assumed, with some sorrow, that I would not have children.

It was a surprise to discover I was pregnant.

In the Quiet: The Demon of Stubbornness, The Angel of Consciousness

Healing sometimes happens when I'm doing other things, just as the creative process continues while there is no visible progress. After the chaos of overwhelm, I move into a period of Incubation.

It looks, sometimes even to me, like I've given up, shelved my efforts at wholeness, or forgotten them. Life offers what looks like an enormous number of distractions and I wander toward them. I plant a garden. I read a book. I take the dog for a walk. I work on a Website. I am not consciously thinking about or working toward healing. I am, off and on, thinking about my illness because it affects how I take action.

I think this is how most people pass their lives and perhaps it's natural and better. Dancing with wholeness is what we organisms do as part of the glorious biological entity of the universe. I choose to be conscious about the dance because that consciousness saves me. Reminding myself that I am moving toward wholeness is the only thing that pulls me out of the morass of overwhelm.

"Can't you just be sick for a while?" asked one of my graduate advisors. I suppose I must have been bitching about how busy I was or how I was struggling physically. I was horrified at her suggestion. It is always in the back of my mind that if I don't do things NOW, I may not be able to do them EVER. I have to get a vegetable garden in now because next year I may not be able to garden at all, even with my new raised beds system. I had to go to Hawaii (grin), because next year the trip may be too much for me.

Taking time out to be sick might be fine if I were going to get over this. I am a little better, lately, at resting if I have a bad headache or cold. But to convalesce with a chronic illness could be permanent.

In the late nineteenth century, it was fashionable to be sick. People like Alice James (sister of Henry, a famous novelist and William, a famous philosopher) spent years in their sickbeds, having guests, writing, advising people. Nowadays such behavior is suspect. Get over it! If you can't be at the gym a couple times a week, you should at least be out of bed and doing things.

I have had, more than once, the almost unforgivable thought that I would rather have a few months of fatal illness than this chronic, anything-that-doesn't-kill-you-outright-makes-you-stronger crap. I could fight heroically, waste away gracefully, plan a great funeral, impress everybody with my good-natured courage. I could sustain that for six months. I've had MS for twenty-five years now and I'm tired of it. I've been running on empty too long. I'm ornery over it way too often.

I keep forgetting the necessity (for me) of surrendering to the damned disease. (Hmm, I may be a little angry about that idea. Of course I am. I don't want to surrender! I want to fight and be courageous. I want to do the hero's journey!)

The problem is that, by fighting, I'm continually pushing down all the bad stuff: the feelings of helplessness, fury, powerlessness and weakness. Guess what happens to everything I push? It gets stronger. I am putting all my "negative" feelings in training against my will. The more often I push, the more muscles I build for them to push back.

I need to soften and surrender. When I use those words, I have in mind a gentle subsidence. That is who I'd like to be (some kind of Hollywoodesque Quaker lady), but that is not who I am. I am so stubborn and so...dramatic...that I can't go gentle into the good night. Surrender in my life looks most often like exhaustion. I have to go and go and go and finally (having paid my dues?) I can give in for a while. Giving in, giving over, giving way. It's sweet.

If I catch my need early enough it can be as simple as a big breath in and a sigh. More often, it's anger followed by tears.

One day, I took our new dog for a walk with Alexis, then four years old. We chose Cora from the shelter because she was a calm dog and not as strong as one of the other dogs we took for a test walk. At forty-five pounds, she was still strong. She saw a squirrel on a neighbor's lawn and went after it, pulling her leash at a sudden right angle to me and my scooter. Wham! I was down on my side with the scooter on top of me. Cora was straining at the end of her line. Alexis, terrified, ran the half block home to get Daddy to help. When Ralph righted me, we continued our walk. I was thinking, I suppose, about getting back on a horse that had thrown me. Who knows?

It was the first sunny day after a long spell of rain. The park was full of picnickers, many of whom had dogs with them. Keeping Cora calm was a tussle. The playground had become a water park, the equipment surrounded by a pool four inches deep. The kids were having a grand time with the water slides and splash-swings created by the flood. We went back home to get Lex's swimming suit.

I took a few moments in the bathroom to cry. "I think I'm hurt," I needed to sob, crying partly with the shock of the collision and partly because I couldn't tell if my ankle, which had been squeezed between the scooter and the curb, was broken or bruised or battered. I can't feel my lower legs or feet. Part of the crying was grieving.

If I remind myself to surrender to my emotions and my body on a regular basis I do better. I am less ornery. I feel less weak. I am taking better emotional care of myself and that results in taking better physical care. When I was a year old, one of my developmental tasks was to learn to walk. I stood. I leaned forward and my feet moved to catch me. It was an unconscious imperative. Now life is inviting me to another stage of development. As an adult, I get to be conscious about it. It is time I lean forward and let healing catch me.

Mother and Artist

In the afternoon of September 9, 1997, I suspect I am in labor. Ralph comes home and I take the walker for a stroll. I have read that if exercise causes labor pains to decrease, it's "false labor." My pains increase. We call the hospital, but they are in no hurry to admit this first-time mother. We arrive at the hospital at ten p.m. The nurse examines me and sends Ralph out to park the car. "We'll try not to have the baby until you get back," she says. Two hours later, we are the delighted parents of a baby girl.

I slept after the birth and woke up feeling tired, but excited. The nurse helped me to the bathroom with my walker and then, a minute later, was calling my name as I sat on the toilet. I thought I had fallen asleep for a minute. She thought I had a small seizure. I spent the morning undergoing an MRI and EEG. My neurologist visited to report that they showed I had MS. While I was peeved at having spent my daughter's first morning away from her so my doctor could confirm a diagnosis I never questioned, I was relieved nothing else had been discovered. We took Alexis home the next day.

While I was pregnant, we had visited a physical therapist at a local center for people with disabilities. She helped us strategize about how I could care for an infant. We bought a sturdy carriage so I could put Alexis in it and use its handles like a walker. I used baby slings to help hold her as I moved short distances or rode on my scooter. Ralph was very involved in her care, giving baths and changing diapers. After a few weeks, we each worked part-time schedules. After a few months, Alexis went to a child care center while we returned to work full time.

Full time for entrepreneurs is rarely forty hours a week. I resented my time away from Alexis and gave the business to my partner. I was able to get a temporary thirty-hour-a-week position doing Web design at a local insurance company.

Having a child gave the monsters a new sound track for their dance. I was unsuccessful at breastfeeding. I didn't feel my bathing her would be safe. Once we used formula, Ralph took over nighttime feedings because lack of sleep seemed to affect me so much more than it did him. I kept expecting to return to walking with a cane, but couldn't seem to manage. (Now, I look back longingly on those first two years when I was able to get down on the floor, play with Alexis and then get back up!) The monster voices in my head chanted that I was a terrible mother.

After Alexis was born, I began taking "MS-modifying" medication. In my case, this was a self-administered weekly injection. The drugs had been available for a couple years, but I heard stories about people who used them feeling ill most of the time. They were designed to slow the progression of the disease. To me, the choice seemed to be: feel good now and worse later or bad now and bad later. I thought some good feelings seemed preferable. Avonex, a newer drug, was injected weekly. I thought one day per week of flu-like symptoms seemed acceptable. And, in some people, the side effects lessened over time. (That has not been the case for me. Some "shot days" are better than others, but they are never wonderful.)

Having given up my entrepreneurial identity and feeling like a loser as a mom, I searched for something to do that would give me a measure of comfort. I became a protégée in a two-year artists mentoring program for women. I met with my mentor once a month and painted for several hours each week. Practicing painting, I danced with my monsters rather than wrestling with them. A vague idea drew me to the blank canvas. Critical voices clamored as soon as I made a mark, but hushed as I focused on the work. Making marks, making mistakes, moving past the monster hubbub to the next mark, we danced. Ideas for the next piece drew me past the dangerous moment when one piece was done and the monsters held up their critical scorecards.

The art world, I found, was structured in favor of my monsters: submit slides for a show; get rejected. Though I love the process of making art, it felt incomplete to tuck it away unseen by the world.

"I hate this whole thing with the slide submissions. I hate the way the art world works," I whined to my mentor.

"How would you like it to work?" she asked.

"I just want people to see the work," I answered. "I want to work in words as well as images. I want the art to be part of their everyday lives." Thinking about this, I found my answer. I offered to do a Lenten art series for the church I was attending. Scripture provided the subject matter. I wanted the work to be large to use the spaciousness of the sanctuary. Ralph found and bought a used, large-format printer. I worked on the computer, making collages of stock photos and printing them in panels three feet square. I wrote a poem for each week and read it as the call to worship. The work came to people as part of their normal experience.

My final project for my mentorship was an art installation called "Bricks." It featured an illustration of a woman in a wheelchair with a

poem beside her, printed three by six feet, behind a pile of foam blocks with negative messages printed on them. Viewers were invited to build walls with the blocks and move around or through them.

It's not just the bricks
that keep me away from you
away from life

Sure stairs and narrow passages
get in my way

But they're more often excuses
I use
to avoid the fear

what if I'm not good enough?
what if you don't like me?
what if I'm too different?
what if I'm too much trouble?

it's too late...
I'm too old...
I'm too busy...
I'm too weird...

Mom said...
Dad said...
God wouldn't want...

So I sit here
waiting to be let in
and pretend it's the bricks
that are in my way

Playing to Lose: The Demon of Ambition, The Angel of Faith

I am not a gentle person, though I wish I were. I would like to be the kind of person who, faced with adversity, surrenders to it gracefully and goes about using whatever blessings she has in service to others. "I'm crabby today," a woman said in a meeting. "Though not," she amended, looking over at me, "as crabby as you." Sigh. She's right. It is hard to imagine anyone could be as crabby as I have been lately.

I get crabby when I try to force my life to be what it isn't—or when I spend time measuring the distance between the ideal and the real. I was recently advised to articulate my vision and mission and have a goal in each of these areas: spiritual, intellectual, financial, professional, physical and social/recreational. My crabbiness quotient immediately increased. It took me days to understand that it was connected to the "visioning/goal setting process" upon which my friend was encouraging me to embark.

Now that I've recognized the problem, I am sighing with relief instead of exasperation. Oh, that again: the hero's journey. Strap on your gun, get on your horse and head west to El Dorado! Every day in every way I'm getting better and better! Think and grow rich! Now I get it electronically: work from home, enlarge your p*nis, save up to 80% on dental bills. We construct ourselves around the idea of progress. We slice our lives into portions and want to see each piece improve each year. We believe we can affirm our way to better lives...lives without limits.

The model of triumph over adversity locks me into a helpless, driven cycle of effort, failure and despair. I remember how I loved physical therapy sessions during that second hospitalization. Each day, I noticed strength and balance returning to my body; I knew healing was taking place. I no longer have the "exacerbating-remitting" form of MS. Instead, like many people who have had the disease for years, I have "chronic progressive" MS. I no longer get Sick with a capital S. Rather, each year, I notice I can do less than I did the year before. The health insurance company will no longer pay for me to receive physical therapy. I cannot show consistent, measurable improvement. I no longer fit their heroic health care model. If you live long enough, you will have this experience, too.

Faced with an unending series of losses, faced with the impossibility of living a "normal" life, I have one glorious, incredibly powerful and absolutely unpopular option: I can give in. No amount of effort or action can fix things. That is what incurable means. Oddly enough, though, surrendering to the frustration, pain and deprivation is the best thing I can do for myself. Recently, driving to yet another meeting, I entertained myself by imagining a performance art piece to be part of my funeral. "Get someone from the circus who spins plates on poles," I advised my brother later that day. "She goes up in front and starts spinning a bunch of plates. She keeps them spinning and spinning and then, all of a sudden, she lets go. As the plates come crashing to the ground, she flings her arms in the air and grins triumphantly because that's what it's going to feel like when I die. I will finally be able to STOP!"

Later still, it occurred to me that I don't have to wait until I die to stop. I can surrender right now. I suspect that giving in is wonderful because I am surrendering *to* something. I am, to put it traditionally, relaxing into the arms of God. My belief in and understanding of a higher power waxes and wanes. Times in my life when I have not believed in God have been followed by surrender to the idea that (as I told two clean-scrubbed and faintly-shocked Mormon missionaries the other day) it doesn't matter if there is one or not, I need to believe there is one. I need a God in part because I need the act of giving in to be joyous instead of frightening. When there is a God, I don't need to be heroic because I am not the star of this show. It is a long, grand, story and I am a bit player. (But, as the saying goes, there are no small parts, only small actors.)

Having let go of the need to make everything come out the Way It Ought To Be, I can relax into what is. I can stop pushing myself and pet the dog instead. It is when I think It is Up to Me to Make Things Right that I am at my most horrible. (Just ask anyone who has been around me for the last month!)

Now here's the trick: giving in cannot mean giving up. Despite the fact that the insurance company will not pay for physical therapy, I have to keep exercising. Exercising does not help me make progress, but it does help me make the most of the strength and ability I have. If I exercise, I am more comfortable and capable even if, every year, I can do less and less. I have to keep playing, even though I am bound to lose.

My clients with mental illness were examples, for me, of an alternative to our culture's vision of the hero. Their illness and the stigma attached to it, had robbed them of jobs, income, the support of family and friends, feelings of safety and trust in themselves. Still, there they were, exploring and expressing their gifts, serving those around them. It is the heroism of surrender and persistence.

I've realized recently that practicing surrender in a safe environment is one of the principal reasons I make art. It never, never, ever comes out the way I envisioned it. I start working with a vision pulling me forward, but the material surprises me. My own limitations thwart me. I have to adjust the plan, go with the process and find out what happens. While the end result is not what I had in mind, every piece I make is a startling self-portrait in the moment. I am a better person when I am making art because it is my practice in surrender. It is prayer.

Willful being that I am, I need to surrender and surrender and surrender. No sooner do I breathe a sigh of relief at not having to be the One In Control, than I think of something else I want to try to fix. When Alexis was three, she began taking swimming lessons. When it was time to practice her back float, her head bobbed out of the water, her legs kicked, her arms flailed. Most of the little ones in her class had the same reaction. Floating on my back is one of my favorite things. Supported gently, sound muted, eyes closed—I am released from effort. I had forgotten that such trust is learned.

Here I am, child in God's water, flailing and gasping when all I need to do is stop thrashing, breathe gently and be supported.

Gains and Losses

Suddenly, we are rich. In the middle of my mentorship, Ralph sells his company for what is, for us, a significant amount of money. Financial advisors tell us we will never worry about money again. But, in the midst of this good fortune, my monsters are bellowing songs of guilt and condemnation.

I had been using a scooter for trips of more than a block for about five years. A couple years previously, we installed a lift in our van. It featured a metal arm that swung out of the back of the van. I could strap the scooter to the arm, use the motor to lift the scooter, push the arm to swing the scooter into the van, use my walker to get to the driver's door and then climb into the van. That process had begun to exhaust me. In addition, I worried about my driving. When my "drop-foot" symptom became permanent, I had been fitted with a leg brace on the right side. I would drive by tilting my pelvis to raise my right foot from the gas pedal and I used my left foot on the brake. I was concerned about whether that was a safe solution. Now that we had money, we modified our van, getting a built-in ramp (so I could drive the scooter into the van) and hand controls. We also bought a 1950's rambler and began extensive accessibility renovations: a kitchen with lowered counters, a roll-in shower and an office so I could work from home.

Emotionally and spiritually, I was struggling. After fifteen years of being a couple who connected during long conversations and long walks, my husband and I were not connecting. Long conversations were impossible with a small child in the room. Strolling hand-in-hand or arm-in-harm was difficult when I was seated and operating controls and

Ralph was walking alongside me. Alexis was a wonderful, active toddler and I could not scoop her up when she needed quick intervention or pick her up when she fell in the sand on the playground. Though I enjoyed the time I spent creating art, my work didn't sell. The department at the insurance company where I had been working was reorganized out of existence and my contract position dissolved. I felt a failure in every area of my life. I was, the monsters sang, a bad wife, bad mom, bad artist, unable to support myself and, underneath it all, a burden who could not pull my own weight. It would be better, came the chorus, if I had died in childbirth.

Down the Rabbit Hole

Once upon a time, there was a rabbit named Innana. She was hopping along happily when she fell into a deep hole. At first she wasn't worried. In her youth she had won some hopping contests and, even though she was no longer young, she remembered her technique. She put her weight on her strong back feet, held her elbows back and close to her body, imagined energy coiling inside her and launched herself into the air. Her first attempt wasn't high enough to make an escape but, undaunted, she tried again. And again. And again. Before long, she was exhausted and her best effort had not even allowed her to see the flat ground outside the hole. She threw herself on the muddy bottom of the hole and wept. Innana had her pride, though and eventually she dried her tears and considered her situation. The walls of her prison were rough with stones and roots. Perhaps she could climb out. Rabbits are better hoppers than climbers, but desperate times call for desperate measures. Innana studied the vertical terrain and plotted an ascent. She practiced holding her paws so that her claws stuck out as much as possible. And she began to climb.

She thought, for a while, that she might make it. Using a clever combination of teeth, front claws, scrambling back feet and moving from rocks to roots to indentations in the dirt, she made it more than halfway up. Then she hit a slippery spot and tumbled to the bottom of the pit. Reminding herself that nobody likes a quitter, she tried again. And again. And again. No matter what route she took, no matter what variations in movement she tried, she would reach a point where the walls defeated her and she fell back to the bottom.

She wept. She snarled. She ran in tight circles. Then, panting and dry eyed, she sprawled in the muddy weeds at the bottom of the hole.

"Can't hop over it," she muttered, remembering a chant she sang as a kit, "Can't climb up it. Gotta dig through it." Rabbits are better hoppers than diggers, but Innana began to dig. She made herself a small cave near the floor of the hole and crawled inside it and slept. She was too exhausted to worry, too tired to think, too weary to move.

In the morning, when the sun was high enough to bring some slanting light into the hole, Innana stirred. She felt a twisting sensation in her stomach. Her sleep-sogged mind slowly replayed the events of yesterday and she shot upright, her whole body quivering. Now that she was rested, she was hungry and if she couldn't escape from the hole, she would surely starve. For a few minutes, she hopped and scrabbled against the walls, desperate to escape. Again, tiredness forced her to calm down and reconsider.

She noticed that there were some clumps of vegetation growing toward the center of the hole where the sunshine reached the pit floor. In fact, she realized, there were some wildflowers there. She went to the plants, bit off a stalk and nibbled down it, saving the succulent flower head for last. Before long, she had eaten an excellent breakfast.

She began to dig, making a side tunnel from her cave that headed toward a memory of a sloping patch of ground where she hoped her tunnel would emerge. After several hours, she stopped for a rest and a snack and so it continued for the entire day. The next day, she dug again, though not with as much dedication. She found herself taking time to watch the clouds and clean her fur, activities she had enjoyed before she had fallen down the pit.

As time went on, Innana found herself digging less and watching clouds more. In fact, some days when she meant to dig, she carved designs into the walls rather than extending the tunnels. She missed eating vegetables and hopping over bushes. Sometimes she missed those things so much and the limitations of her life seemed so harsh that she spent time huddled on the floor of the hole weeping. But eventually the sadness would subside. It was not the life she once had led and she was not the rabbit she once had been, but there were clouds to watch, wildflowers to nibble and designs to carve. It was enough and so was she.

Creative Experiments in Incubation

Rules Review:

1. Use the materials and spaces of your choice: fancy or plain, special or ordinary, comfortable or challenging. It may help to pretend you're a little kid.

2. Do what you like (or change it so you *do* like it) and leave the rest.

3. Just once, try doing the one that seems most outside your comfort zone.

4. Be gentle with yourself.

5. Have fun.

Writing Starters:

Write the starter words and then keep going, keeping the words coming one after another even if you're writing "I don't know what to say next, but if I did...".

- I fight my situation when…

- I give in when…

- I escape by…

- Being in control…

- Being out of control…

- I can't give in because…

- Giving in isn't giving up when…

- I could be a hero by…

- I can't be a hero because

- *Be about to write (hold your writing utensil above the paper or your fingers poised above the keyboard) for two full minutes.*

- Healing, for me, is…

- Once upon a time…

Making your Mark:

With the mark-making utensils of your choice (color adds meaning and fun), make marks in response to the suggestion. Be as sketchy—or as elaborate—as you want to be.

- Make triumphant marks.

- Make defeated marks.

- Make controlled and ambitious marks, then chaotic and helpless marks.

- *Be about to draw (hold your mark-making utensil above the surface) for two full minutes.*

Objects in Space:

Find a flat surface you can use for these experiments. You need to be able to leave it, have it be undisturbed, and come back to it the next day. Find household or run-of-the-mill objects or make your own.

- Choose ten objects and put them on the edges of the surface. Imagine moving them into an arrangement that satisfies you. Do not move them. Repeat this experiment in a day or two.

Sounding it Out:

Start with a rhythm—clap or tap on a surface. Add a repetitive sound—pitch, volume and duration are up to you. If you're a musician, feel free to use an instrument. If you're "not a musician," use your voice and body to make noise. Break free of the repetition and experiment.

- Sound like triumph over.

- Sound like yielding to.

- Sound like freedom from.

- Sound like germination.

- Sound like possibility.

- Be as silent as you can be for five minutes.

So the Drama:

Set up two empty chairs, facing each other. As you change roles, move from one chair to the other. Feel free to get up and move around. If someone unexpected shows up, add a chair.

- Your swaggering, heroic self discusses tactics with your tired, surrendered self. Are there monsters and/or angels in the room?

Move Through it:

Make your body into a pose representing the idea: adjust your facial expression, how you hold your head and torso, how you position your arms and legs. Once you have the pose, begin to move out of it. Let how fast you move, how you move and how you're using the space grow from the idea.

- You are an ice sculpture on a warm day. Is this a story of defeat or homecoming?

Part Four: Reconciliation

Alive and Together

The Reverend Laurie waves the sheet of paper I have given her in the air.

"Do you realize how CONTROLLING this is?" she asks.

The paper is my plan for my "weak and helpless" day, an assignment that is part of a six-month personal growth program in which I'm participating. Laurie replaces my breakfast plans of fruit and granola with eggs and bacon. Rather than staying at home, I will be carried to the second floor of a classmate's house. Classmates will bathe me, feed me and read me stories. The underlying philosophy is that everything that seems to happen to me is my idea. My thoughts are creating my reality. On some level, I want to be disabled. If I change my thought patterns, my teachers suggest, perhaps my illness will shift, too. They make no promises, but tell stories of other students who have experienced health improvements.

There were things that were wonderful about the program. I came to understand that my judgments about myself and others were just that: passing ideas that didn't necessarily reflect any truth. I practiced identifying and challenging negative beliefs. I practiced deep breathing techniques and received massage, chiropractic treatments and acupuncture. My classmates shared their life stories and current struggles with me with great honesty. I appreciated the magnificence that is each individual in a new way.

On the other hand, the program was devastating. Teachers were understood to be absolutely right and my teachers decided that Ralph was an angry, emotionally unavailable unbeliever. I should leave him. In January, we separated after eighteen years of marriage. I moved to an apartment with a classmate. Alexis, who was three, spent part of the week with each of us. Ralph was traveling extensively for his new job. The new house was still torn apart for remodeling; in some ways, it felt good to be away. It was during this time that I gave up the low-fat diet regimen I had been using for almost twenty years. I was acting, my teachers said, out of fear and a desire to punish myself. I should let those go.

With so much attention focused on my physical state, I was watching for improvement and seemed to see it. I thought I was able to flex my right ankle slightly. (Looking back, it's not clear to me if this was a new ability or a new awareness of a not-much-used ability.)

Part of the separation was my own version of a temper tantrum. I thought of it (in a mostly subconscious way) as a wake-up call to Ralph. I wanted more attention. I wanted more emotional intimacy. I wanted my wanting to be taken seriously. One of my classmates was also dealing with chronic illness. When he died, I realized I was wasting precious time. I did not want was to be away from Ralph and Alexis. (But, coward that I am, neither did I want to put up with my teachers' criticism of our relationship.) . As soon as the program was over in May, I moved back in and we set about a tentative rebuilding of our family. I was alive and should focus on living, not on dodging the effects of illness.

On Asking for Help: The Demon of Self-Sufficiency, The Angel of Vulnerability

Living with chronic illness teaches me about asking for help. I am still not good at it. I wonder if there is a culture on earth where asking for help is considered good. In America, we are supposed to be rugged individualists, able to handle things ourselves, invigorated by challenge.

My response to being overwhelmed by illness is to curl up in a ball and pretend to be nobody. If this were physical, it would be easier to spot. Instead, I hunker down spiritually and emotionally. It's so subtle I don't even realize at first that I'm doing it. I isolate myself and build strong invisible walls to keep myself safe from attack. This also keeps me safe from rescue.

It makes sense to me that I try to protect myself this way but, ironically, it's exactly the wrong thing to do. What I need is to connect with someone. At the very least, I need to pick up the phone and talk to someone. Better, I need to meet face to face. I'm not talking about counseling sessions, but neither am I talking about chatting in line at the grocery store.

I don't always have to pour my heart out, but I do need to admit I have one. My first experience of this came at Emotions Anonymous. The twelve steps gave me a practical agenda and a sense of progress that satisfied my thirst for achievement while the content of the steps taught me to trust. What really mattered was that a group of former strangers sat around and talked about our emotional lives. We admitted we were not the together, self-sufficient folks we might appear. It was impossible to sustain my John Wayne act during a twelve-step meeting.

Twenty years later, I am realizing the importance of moving those kinds of relationships into my everyday life. When I am scared or grieving or angry, it is time to ask for help. The hardest part is to realize that I am not a total reject for feeling this way—that asking someone for help is not the most horrible thing I could do.

During my "weak and helpless" day in the personal growth program, I was not allowed to do anything for myself. Perfectly able-bodied students in the program also had such days. It was meant to teach me that receiving help is OK…that people are happy to give…that giving and receiving are the same thing. Right after that day I felt softer, less fierce. I am glad I did it.

Some of the softness from my weak and helpless day carried over into my "real life," but not much. There was that suggestion that if I truly felt my weak and helpless feelings, I would not "need" to be sick. When people suggest I am sick by choice, I get angry. I don't entirely disagree with the thought, but I get angry nonetheless.

I am angry about being ill. I am angry that I got MS in the first place. I am angry that my efforts at clean living have not been rewarded with good health, or at least one of those "hardly know you have it" versions of the disease. I am angry that I have to ask for help. I'm angry that, often, when I ask, I don't get help. I'm angry that I can't do so many things. I'm angry that I can't run and walk and sit on the floor with my child. I'm angry that many well-meaning people have ideas about things I could try that will, they hope, cure me. I am angry that some people think I shouldn't be angry about it. I am angry that some people think that my anger (or any other mental/emotional/physical action I'm taking) is causing the disease.

This anger is part of me. If I try to deny it or repress it, it just comes out sideways all over the place. In my twenties and early thirties, I took it inside and felt unworthy to take up space on the planet. I became depressed and wanted to die. More recently, I've been angry toward other people. I imagine, in my monster-mind, that if they offered me more (or different) support, my life would be much easier.

When I am most sane, I realize (sometimes even in advance) that something will be hard for me and ask someone to help me. "Would you please pick up that box from the floor and set it on the counter?" It's fairly easy and works well.

I like to think that I wouldn't be slow to ask for help if I didn't need help so often. That's probably an excuse. Another one I use is that I don't know I need help until I've tried it a few times myself. There's a shard of truth there: sometimes I think I might be able to do something and have to discover, through experimentation, whether I can. Nine times out of ten, though, I can predict whether I'm likely to need help and always it is easier when I have help.

If I think, "with a bit more effort, I can get this box from the floor," I will try it. My left hand is on the scooter handle, keeping me from falling over. My right hand slides the box to the scooter and then pushes the box against the scooter and up, lifting slowly. Once I get the top of the box to the level of the scooter seat, with the bottom of the box still only inches off the floor, it falls before I can get my hand under it. I try again. Same results. I try again. It falls again.

"Would you like some help?" Ralph asks.

I click my tongue. "Yes," I snarl.

My greatest fear is that I am a burden to those around me. My disability, after all, causes them massive inconvenience and sets them apart from their peers. If I'm always asking for help, it will wear on people. No one will want to be around me. I will be a "high maintenance wife" in the worst and truest sense of that expression.

I've noticed that people like to help at their own convenience and at predictable intervals. It would be nice if I could say to my husband, for instance, "I'm going to fall next week. Would Thursday at ten work for you to come pick me up off the floor or do you have a meeting that morning? If you're busy, I'll reschedule." But of course, that's not how it works! It seems inevitable that I have a near fall in the bathroom and am clinging to a grab bar calling for help at the same moment as Alexis finds a spider in her bedroom and starts screaming. Ralph is constantly making choices, based on volume and pitch, about who is in more trouble. It's not always easy to tell.

All of my cultural roles come with an element of "helper" built into them. As wife, mother, community volunteer, coworker and teacher, others are supposed to be able to ask me for help and be pretty sure I will provide it. (Or, more likely, I am there to anticipate their needs and provide the help without their asking for it.) If I can't give them what they need or, worse, if I have to ask them for help, it's easy for me to imagine I can't fulfill the role. I spent the first two years of Alexis' life with an internal refrain that "I am a bad mother." (Sometimes I escalated it to "horrible" and "terrible" just to increase my punishment and assuage my guilt.) There was so much I couldn't do—or that it was safer for Ralph to do—for the baby. Anybody can love a baby. That's easy. So that can't be of much value. It's the bathing her and holding her hands while she practices walking and spotting her while she's on the playground that matter. Of course, I know that's not true. But my monster-mind is powerful and convincing. If I can't be a cheerful helper at all times, what use am I?

As a visible minority, I'm always afraid I'll blow it for the home team. If I ask for help, others will think that people with disabilities are helpless and whiny. If I am, on the other hand, getting through those heavy double doors without help, observers will think that people with disabilities are competent and creative.

Needing help is a frequent condition of small children. It's easy, then, to assume that someone who needs help shares other qualities of children. I see this all the time in the way we treat elders. Someone who is "old and feeble" and, therefore, needs help cleaning her house or even getting to the bathroom must also need help handling her money and deciding what clothes to wear. It's confusing, of course, because some people who are elderly or disabled do have conditions that affect their ability to reason and make decisions. But even then, we are not children.

Many people who are elderly or disabled share something else: loss. We used to be able to do these things. Sometimes we don't even know until we're halfway into them that we no longer can do them. Of course we'll try again, rather than asking for help! It's hard to imagine the change has come about. When did that happen? And, there, in the middle of trying to accomplish something, we are awash in grief in all its majesty: disbelief, anger, bargaining...all of it, right there, in that moment. We have no resources left to be asking for help.

There are rafts of reasons for me to resist asking for help and, it often seems, only weakness and laziness in favor of asking. One simple thing tips the balance: I need help. The fact is that I cannot step up on the scale, cannot lift the child from the bathtub, cannot fold brochures for an hour. It is the same "cannot" as I used to experience as an able-bodied person when I could not reach a high shelf or get the cap off a new jar of peanut butter. It is beyond my physical capabilities. But while I felt no shame for being short or needing help with tight lids, I am ashamed of the kind of help I need now. And that is the problem.

If I could strip the emotional baggage away from my moment of need, it would be easy to ask for help. But I am a human being and, as such, every moment is rich in emotion. What I need to do, I suspect, is recognize the baggage and make an internal gesture that releases it. Set the emotions aside and consider the facts: I can't do this. or I am uncertain I can do it, or it may be dangerous for me to attempt it without "a spotter." I can, at least, try that as an experiment.

My sane mind is free of blame and accusation. When the anger arises and I am sane, I can watch it rise and dissipate without attachment. Breathe in. Breathe out. Watch it fade. Understand that I am a human animal with emotions and being angry or in need does not make me evil. Breathe in. Breathe out. Notice that I am alive.

Building Support

I make it a personal priority to build an emotional support system. I go to a twelve-step support group, find a more vibrant church and participate in artists' groups. I have mushy boundaries, so it's difficult for me to be part of something without pouring so much into it that I become resentful. I try to find a middle ground, but I'm not very successful.

When we moved into the house, I promised myself that I would use my scooter less and my walker more, but I didn't keep my promise. Using the scooter, I could move around the house; I could clean; I could cook. Using the walker was exhausting and felt unsafe. For a while, I received physical therapy, but I wasn't making any progress and that was when the insurance company decided not to pay for more.

Meanwhile, Ralph's employer folded out from under him and he wasn't finding a new position. It was a strange time. Our house was beautiful and conveniently accessible. We lived a half block from a lake. We added raised garden beds in the yard. Alexis had good friends relatively close by. But our savings was disappearing down the drain of unemployment. The money we'd given our financial advisors had been lost in the stock market. I was working as a freelance Web designer but wasn't making a living. Ralph was offered a job in California and it seemed sensible to take it. California weather and public transportation would be more appropriate for a person with disability. "You'll feel better in California," promised a friend who had lived there.

Separating Body and Mind: The Demon of Analysis, the Angel of Uncertainty

During the nineteenth century, separating body from mind and understanding them as mechanisms helped humankind find cures and treatments for a range of ills. During the twentieth century, we began to suspect we had made a mistake and played around with the idea of "holistic medicine." To help ourselves, we need flexible models.

I was driving a coworker to her doctor's appointment. She was a mess. She had a cold she couldn't seem to shake. Her marriage was coming apart. She was a thousand miles away from her extended family and old friends. She leaned her head against the window of my car and moaned, "I feel terrible and I don't know if it's physical or emotional."

"I'm not sure," I remember suggesting cautiously, "that it really matters."

We were both working at the drop-in center for people diagnosed with mental illness. Around us we saw people in all sorts of physical and emotional distress. Some of them were part of the "bio-brain association," a group organized around the idea that mental illness is solely the result of chemical imbalances in the brain. Most people I knew who were members joined as an argument against the notion that the source of their illness was some attitude or action they or their parents took or didn't take. Our center was founded with the idea that people could recover from mental illness the same way they recover from alcoholism. Recovery, under that model, is a lifetime process. Our emphasis was not on how people came to find themselves ill, but how they could cope on the other side of the diagnosis.

"We have not found it helpful," says my favorite twelve-step literature, "to place labels on any degree of illness or health." Living with a chronic illness of still-mysterious origin, I find it serves me best to be vague about the relationship between my body and my mind. When I was first diagnosed, a nurse observed that most patients she saw with MS exacerbations had gotten worse following a stressful event or period in their lives. I lived very carefully for the next ten years. I studied meditation, biofeedback and yoga. I turned down invitations to participate in weddings and worked part time. My MS came and went, seemingly unrelated to the rise and fall of stress in my life. I discovered that the mind-body connection cannot be described in simple terms.

During the nineteenth century, René Descartes tried to make humans as clean and certain as mathematics by suggesting that the rational soul is an entity distinct from the body. Body could affect mind when an outflow of "animal spirits" rearranged the nervous system. Through voluntary action, the soul could make a difference in the outflow of animal spirits; mind could affect body.

My family was, without ever saying it, staunchly Cartesian. Intellect set us apart from the animals. The body was an inefficient mechanism used to transport our brains, which is where our value lay. I grew up not realizing that understanding body separate from mind is a philosophical position. I thought it was The Truth.

Growing up, my body wasn't an ally. I have early memories of rolling down hills laughing with pleasure, but I wasn't a standout physical specimen. I never learned to throw or catch a ball. I didn't know it was a skill to be learned. I thought other kids could do it and I couldn't. For a few years, I thought I might be pretty: my hair was long and straight and parted in the center—stylish in the late sixties. As I grew, my breasts didn't and my nose did. I was firmly convinced, by the time I was ten, that my only salvation would come from being smart.

I could demonstrate smart and make a case for artistically talented. I did well on any test involving pencil and paper, was cast in plays and won music awards. For a kid trying to prove herself, recognition was essential. No way could I look like one of Charlie's Angels (even the smart one), but I could hold my own in debate club and make good grades. My body—the other—carried my mind (the "real" me) around.

After Descartes, philosophers spent the next two hundred years arguing over the relationship of the brain/mind/body. God is in charge, suggested some. Body doesn't affect mind, nor does mind affect body. If I decide to move my finger and I move my finger, it's only because God decided the finger should be moved. My decision had nothing to do with it. Or maybe my finger and my mind are different aspects of God and both decision and motion are the divine at work. Maybe my thought doesn't cause the movement at all; they just happen in sequence. Maybe God set it up that way to begin with. Maybe God and thought are both illusions and the finger just moves. The philosophical wrangling goes on endlessly and I get bored with the whole thing.

What I really want to know is: is there anything I can do to feel healthy? The answer is, as near as I can tell, unknowable. With a few phone calls, I can have people lined up around the block with suggestions for me, but nobody has a sure thing. So, if I set the question of cure aside, as gently and blamelessly as possible, what's next?

Does how I think affect my physical health? The answer is yes. It's simple common sense that when I feel happy and positive, I feel more physical energy and less pain. When I allow the alternative health advocates to provide services to me I do, in fact, feel better for a while. Their confident hope, combined with my tendency to want to please people, makes me believe that I feel better. Their hopes fade as my measurable symptoms remain unchanged. Their excitement and interest wane, as does my bank balance. I decide to try to generate my own good feelings for less money.

Our language locks us into the body/mind split. The only way I can sidestep the issue is to talk about "the organism," and that word distances me from all that is me. Distancing is the problem I'm trying to overcome by looking for an alternative model. About fifteen years ago, when my tendency to drag my right foot did not go away, even as other symptoms of an exacerbation subsided, I surprised myself by bursting into tears while hitting at my right leg. It was the one causing problems, after all. I was fine. My body had betrayed me and my right leg was the ringleader. I trained myself away from calling it "my bad leg," but, even now, I find myself talking about "that right leg" or "the right leg" instead of *my* right leg.

Hope is hidden beneath this linguistic tangle. I'm trying to separate myself from my sick body because I recognize that I am whole and unharmed. During my third exacerbation, I was moving with great difficulty. I determined to do one thing each day: wash the dishes. I remember leaning, exhausted, against the kitchen counter, standing on the brown indoor-outdoor carpet. I was washing a cup, but my attention was on the fear of disability I felt crowding close around me like the oppressive heat before a summer thunderstorm on the prairie. With a sort of internal gesture, I brought my attention back to washing the cup. Rippled stoneware texture. Tan cup with blue stripe near the rim. Warm sudsy water. Laminate counter biting slightly into my hips as it helped me stay standing. Suddenly the fear lifted. I had a sense that everything was all right. Everything would be all right. Not that I would get well, or even live, but that there was nothing to fear. No matter what happened, I would not be harmed. It is the nearest I have come to seeing God.

The more I recognize that my physical body is not the whole me, the more I feel myself a part of it, the healthier I feel. If I can get away from the "courageous me vs. betraying body" illusion, I feel better. Every moment, the disease exists within me—signals end in sparks across scarred nerve sheaths. Every moment, health exists within me—a hundred processes are safely enacted. My food digests; my eyes blink; my brain emits chemicals that end in a smile. I am at least as healthy as I am ill, but I often recognize only my illness.

Taking arms against a sea of troubles didn't work out well for Hamlet. My early determination to fight my disease was similarly ill-fated. Battling against my disease too easily becomes hating my body. If Hamlet had said, "make sail against a sea of troubles and by harnessing such power, go beyond them," he might have transcended his conflicts. Language both demonstrates thought and invites it.

I am most generous to myself when I live in the murky uncertainty of being a whole organism. It doesn't serve me to separate my body from myself, my right foot from my left, or even illness from health. My job is to accept and celebrate myself as I am, to take actions I know will make me feel better, whether that means exercise, attending a support group or forgiving myself for doing neither. My body is me and I am more than my body. It is a glorious paradox.

Firing the Orchestra

"I have a seven year old daughter," I tell the Californian neurologist. "I want ten more years to live at home and be a mom. I'm not sure I'm going to make it." I have driven my scooter the three blocks to the clinic. We have chosen our apartment well: It is within "scootering" distance to almost everything. I take the van out once a week to drive to church. I'm not working and am enjoying spending extra time with Alexis and her friends. I'm consciously building memories.

"There's a new treatment we can try," the neurologist replies. He explains that a drug called Novantrone, usually used for cancer chemotherapy, is being tried for MS. It will allow me to escape the weekly cycles of my "MS-modifying" injection. Quarterly bouts of flu-like symptoms sound better. I agree to give it a try.

The intravenous treatments of shockingly blue fluid weren't too bad. They weren't followed (for me) by terrible nausea. They were followed, however, by vaginal bleeding and, by the time I received my third treatment, dangerously low white blood cell counts that took too long to recover. I wore a facemask for a couple weeks and worried about survival. We decided to stop the treatment. Later I read Dr. Jerry Wolinsky's explanation: "The disease-modifying drugs regulate the immune system in a way that appears to correct some of the abnormalities that may be fundamental to MS progression. I think of it as changing the conductor to make the orchestra sound better....Chemotherapy is more like firing the whole orchestra and hoping that management hires a new group of players who won't make the same mistakes." My orchestra's players are still hitting wrong notes.

I had left for California with high hopes for a calmer, healthier, more environmentally-sound life. One of our first days there, in December, we visited a park in Mountain View. The trees and grass were a lush green. There were few people in the park, but many fearless black squirrels. One of them climbed up the back of the scooter and scurried away in shock when I yelped. (They are used to stealing snacks from unoccupied baby strollers.) Alexis learned to pump herself on a swing that day. I felt a sense of expansive excitement. We found an apartment next to Caltrain and half a block from downtown Sunnyvale's farmer's market.

Over the next two years, we built a new life, though not the one for which I'd hoped. We found a church; Alexis found friends. I loved being able to scooter almost everywhere. But there was a cultural undertow, in Silicon Valley, that didn't fit for us. It seemed to be about ambition, accomplishment and money. We should have Alexis in a private school, people thought. She should be swimming and dancing competitively. We should be collecting a portfolio of her work so we could get her into a gifted and talented program. Church meetings were mostly about money for capital improvements. Conversations with other moms were about ambitions for children or financial strategizing. (I have to admit, I was focused on money, too. We were paying more per month for our two-bedroom apartment than we had in house payments. We were living in California on a Minnesota salary.)

A few months after my flirtation with chemotherapy treatment, we moved back to Minnesota. We returned to friends and family and weather and culture that suit us. We were not, of course, able to return to our old house and neighborhood. While some things are familiar, others are new and driving through our "old" neighborhood brings pangs of grief and regret.

As I write this, we are living in a one-level rental town home and I am struggling with new physical losses. I am not able to transfer reliably and sometimes fall getting to or from the driver's seat or toilet. My hands and arms are becoming increasingly affected: weak and shaky. How long will it be safe for me to be left alone in the house? How long will I be able to drive to work? How long will I be able to work? There are no answers.

I have declared this year one of "disability planning:" to find out what services are available to prolong my independence and minimize my burden on my family. Initial research is not encouraging.

Myrna's Search for Meaning

Once upon a time, there was a princess named Myrna. She was the third daughter of the king of Flootania, a backwater Kingdom on the edge of a forgotten continent.

You may have noticed how third sons of kings often star in fairy tales. Their older brothers, portrayed as strong and intelligent, get the throne and the chancellorship, respectively and the youngest prince is left to seek adventure and deal with witches and dragons.

Being the third *daughter* of a king is even worse. Myrna's oldest sister was given in marriage to the prince of the large country to the East and her next sister was given in marriage to a duke in the middle–sized country to the North. Since Flootania has impassible swamps to the South and a large ocean to the West, this left Myrna with limited options.

By the time our story gets rolling, Myrna is thirty-six. She has cut the ribbons on enough shopping malls and smashed bottles over the prows of enough ships and thrown the puck out for enough mriffle–hockey games to last her a lifetime and a half. Alternatively, she's had enough madcap adventures trying to run away in the swamps and been the subject of enough Royal Inquiries into the Disturbance in His Majesty's Court (such as the one designed to discipline her for writing "I don't deserve this" on the bottoms of the shoes of someone who, half an hour later, knelt to be knighted) to have shaved a dozen years off her life expectancy. Things are looking grim.

On this rainy Monday morning, Myrna is in the Palace Library looking for a solution to her Problem. If you asked her, very politely, what that problem might be, she would turn graciously and regally and snarl out, "I have no prospects, no future, no abilities and I'm getting old!"

Myrna is in the section of the library containing books of advice to princesses. She has passed over books of etiquette, books of grooming, books of language study, music study and needlework study and is squatting down to see the lowest shelf in the darkest corner. There she finds a tiny, green book with gold embossed letters reading, *If You're Out of Options.*

She pulls it out and tries to open it, but it is as if the pages have been glued together. Back at a library table, Myrna struggles mightily trying to open the book. She grabs both edges and pulls. She pries at it with her fingernails. (Snap) She pulls out her Swiss army knife (even princesses in fairy tales should have one) and tries to cut the book open. It might as well be made of stone.

Myrna hurls the book to the floor in frustration. She takes a deep breath and screams, "Zeldaaaaa!"

With a sprinkle of twinkling lights and a small puff of smoke, Myrna's fairy godmother appears. Now, all princesses have fairy godmothers, but being fairy godmother to the youngest princess in a backwater kingdom is not what you'd call a primo position. Myrna's fairy godmother is a small, wizened old woman in a dirty calico dress and an even dirtier apron reading "Never trust a skinny cook." She is smoking a cigar, but takes it out of her mouth long enough to say, "You rang, Your Highness?"

"Yeah, Zelda, I want to get this book open."

Zelda rolls her eyes. "I'm holding a pair of tens and this schlemiel wants a book opened!" she says to no one in particular. Zelda waddles over to the library table, picks up the book and examines it. She puffs cigar smoke on it and it changes quickly to a toad, an eagle, a surprised-looking Sigmund Freud and back to a book. She shakes her head sadly and looks at Myrna with great compassion. "Nope, sorry, honey, I can't do it." Then she brightens, "I know!" she squeals delightedly, "Why don't you take a bookbinding class!" Her eyes lose their focus for a minute. "Oops! Sorry, gotta go. It's my deal."

Well, Myrna is downcast, but she is, at heart, an obedient creature. She trots off to her room and hauls out the Flootania Community Education catalog, finds herself a bookbinding class and enrolls. She learns about combination presses, single signatures and headbands. She shows the little green book to her class and her teacher and they are all fascinated, but no one can open it.

Myrna has gotten her teeth into this, though and she refuses to give in. She goes on to take Bookbinding II and Advanced Bookbinding Techniques. She learns about acid migration, bosses, rectos and vellum. Pretty soon Myrna is spending most of her time in the Center for Book Art, practicing what she's learned. Every time she meets a new expert, she shows them her book and every time they are unable to tell her how to open it.

Months pass. Myrna attends regional bookbinding conferences. She travels to different cities, meets people, listens to interesting lectures, tries new and exciting bookbinding techniques. She develops a close personal relationship with a calligrapher at the Center for Book Art.

Years pass. Through her new contacts, Myrna has developed interests in calligraphy, art, folk dancing, gourmet cooking and breeding Maltasian turf rabbits.

One night when Myrna and her calligrapher sweetheart are sitting in front of the fire relaxing, Zelda pops in for a visit.

"Hi," she says, putting her feet, clad in size twelve boots, up on the coffee table. "It suddenly occurred to me you haven't called in three years. You in trouble? Look, honey, I know I haven't been too helpful in the past, but I think the world of you. I'm anxious to help."

Myrna looks startled. "Three years?" she asks. "Has it been that long?"

And in a quick running flashback worthy of a Hollywood movie, Myrna thinks about her years as a young, obedient princess, launching ships and shopping malls. She thinks about her years as a rebel princess, running away to the swamps and spitting at high officials. She thinks about recent, happier years when she has not been particularly aware of being a princess at all. And she thinks about the turning point in her life.

All fairy godmothers are a little psychic, which explains why Zelda chooses this moment to say, "Whatever happened to that book?"

"Oh, that," laughs Myrna. "I lost it when I lost my luggage on that trip to the conference in Cincinnati." She turns to her sweetheart, "You remember, honey, that's the conference where..."

And they are lost in reminiscence.

Meanwhile, in a city called Minneapolis in a land far from Flootania, a young flight attendant who has shut herself in the lost luggage room to cry notices an open suitcase, a jumble of clothes and a small green book.

Creative Experiments in Reconciliation

Rules Review:

1. Use the materials and spaces of your choice: fancy or plain, special or ordinary, comfortable or challenging. It may help to pretend you're a little kid.

2. Do what you like (or change it so you *do* like it) and leave the rest.

3. Just once, try doing the one that seems most outside your comfort zone.

4. Be gentle with yourself.

5. Have fun.

Writing Starters:

Write the starter words and then keep going, keeping the words coming one after another even if you're writing "I don't know what to say next, but if I did...".

- When I can do it myself...

- When I can't do it myself...

- Asking for help...

- I'm most vulnerable when...

- When I understand something...

- When I don't understand something...

- My body...

- My mind…
- My spirit…
- My soul…
- Healing, for me, is…
- Once upon a time…

Making your Mark:

With the mark-making utensils of your choice (color adds meaning and fun), make marks in response to the suggestion. Be as sketchy—or as elaborate—as you want to be.

- Make strong, independent marks.
- Make vulnerable, dependent marks.
- Make two very different types of marks combine.
- Make two very different types of marks create something new.

Objects in Space:

Find a flat surface you can use for these experiments. You need to be able to leave it, have it be undisturbed, and come back to it the next day. Find household or run-of-the-mill objects or make your own.

- Choose three objects that attract you and three objects that repel you. Arrange them in a way that pleases you. Come back in a day or two and look at the space. Move the objects into a different, but no less pleasing, arrangement.

Sounding it Out:

Start with a rhythm—clap or tap on a surface. Add a repetitive sound—pitch, volume and duration are up to you. If you're a musician, feel free to use an instrument. If you're "not a musician," use your voice and body to make noise. Break free of the repetition and experiment.

- Sound like independence.

- Sound like vulnerability.

- Sound like peace.

- Sound like your body.

- Sound like your mind.

- Sound like your body and mind together.

So the Drama:

Set up two empty chairs, facing each other. As you change roles, move from one chair to the other. Feel free to get up and move around. If someone unexpected shows up, add a chair.

- Your body and whatever parts of you have been ignoring or insulting your body are making peace with each other.

Move Through it:

Make your body into a pose representing the idea: adjust your facial expression, how you hold your head and torso, how you position your arms and legs. Once you have the pose, begin to move out of it. Let how fast you move, how you move and how you're using the space grow from the idea.

- You are trying to lift a heavy load by yourself. After several clever attempts, you give in, ask for help and receive it. Are you relieved or disappointed?

Part Five: Rededication

The Healing Environment: Deterring Demons, Inviting Angels

"A hospital is a horrible place to be when you're not feeling well," my friend reminded me. The doctor had removed her appendix the day before and she was anxious to return home. She described the conditions many of us dread: noisy hallways, sleep interruptions, schedules driven by shift changes rather than patient needs. Wonderful as hospitals are when we need the skilled attention they provide, they don't really support us as we seek to heal.

I nominate two atmospheres as most healing: the Zero Cabinet and the Artist's Studio. Each encourages different parts of the healing process. Neither is common in hospitals.

One type of environment is quiet, serene and spacious. It's exemplified by Japanese architecture and design. There is no clutter; tools and supplies are hidden in cupboards. Colors are subtle. The natural world is often represented with one object. There is silence or sounds are muted. Surfaces are smooth or regularly textured. Tastes and smells are simple. My shorthand name for this space comes from an old BBC TV series, *Dr. Who*. Every now and then (when the star actor moved on to other projects) the Doctor would "regenerate," changing his old body into a new one. At least once, he requested a "zero cabinet" for regeneration. Shut away from distractions, he could take on the work of transforming. In some ways, this environment is restful. There's nothing to do and little to notice. Without other disturbances, we may become aware of our own mental chatter and physical sensations. If we need rest, this environment will allow it; if we need care, this environment will reveal it.

On the opposite end of the spectrum is a setting full of stimulation and invitation, like a Mexican market. Tools and supplies are visible in buckets and cubbies. Colors are riotous. There can be music, conversation and ambient noise. Surfaces, tastes and smells are complex and multi-layered. I recently saw a video of the offices at Pixar animation studios, where cubicles are cottages and castles filled with drawings, toys, artwork, piñatas and reminder signs. This environment of creative chaos invites us to play, to experiment, to move into new territory. In it, we can rediscover and express who we are. We can practice moving forward without knowing what to expect. We can make mistakes and move beyond them. We can be alive.

Regardless of my physical surroundings, my internal environment (my attitude) is significant. I heal best when I am moving toward openness, acceptance, spontaneity, flexibility and relaxation—when I allow myself the freedom to make mistakes. What I'm really saying is that I heal best when I am moving toward healing. Living with the open heart that is the source of those attitudes *is* being healed. I have to say "moving toward" because I have the attitude for a second and then it slips away. When, using Christian language, I say I am a sinner, I am recognizing this process of losing wholeness the moment I touch it. Repentance is recognizing the loss and turning myself back toward God.

Into this healing space, we invite the angels of surrender, discernment, acceptance and encouragement.

We surrender to the healing process. This includes releasing our agenda and our vision of what should happen. We have to give up trying to control the process and instead simply watch it. Each creative process has its own rhythm and timing. We witness the unfolding.

It is helpful, though, to name what is happening and see it from a larger perspective. This combination of recognizing and understanding what's going on is sometimes called "discernment" and it is a powerful ally. For example, if I can first recognize this racing pulse, this pounding head, these short breaths as <u>rage</u> and then realize that this rage is part of my grieving process, I find myself much more able to accept what is happening. Discernment is an area in which we can help each other. It is often easier to see what is happening if we are outside the experience.

Whatever the circumstance, I find acceptance crucial. Refusing to accept my anger gives it more power over me and keeps me stuck. By allowing, we open ourselves to whatever comes. Having recognized and experienced what *is* happening, we open ourselves to—we accept—what *has* happened.

The encouraging part of me holds my trust in the process. It is that part of me that knows that everything is all right, that urges me to accept the gifts enclosed within the healing process. Encouragement does not have to include promises of cure or return to what was. It is, instead, an ability to find joy and meaning in what *is*.

Different movements in the healing dance go better in different spaces. It would be nice to insist that each individual makes the decisions about what environment he or she needs. Unfortunately, I can't always tell what will work for me. If I am hiding from feelings, I move toward the distraction and action of the Mexican market. So much to see! So much to do! How easy it is to dodge my feelings when I am busy. It might be better, though, to spend time in the zero cabinet. It will be hard, there, not to hear the thoughts that reflect (or perhaps generate) the feelings I'm trying to escape. My experience is that healing is a strong and self-correcting process. If I insist on busy-ness, the feelings will show up in an object I make, or in my attitude while I am distracting myself. Choosing the right environment for the moment may make healing go more comfortably. Healing will occur, comfortable or not. Understanding my environment can support or impede it. Understanding that I have a choice about it is part of the healing.

Angel Invitation Number One: Dare to be Different

Perhaps one of the advantages of growing up in The Sixties is that it introduced me to the idea that being different was A Good Thing. Conformity and sameness were nowheresville and being weird was groovy. I always felt different. I felt older and odder than my peers. Older, because my brothers and sister were significantly older than I and I grew up in a household of adults. Odder because of what I will generously call my artistic temperament. I held my differences close like a delightful secret. They made me special.

I was twenty-one the first time I walked with a cane for any length of time and I felt that everyone was staring at me. Some of them stared while trying not to stare, which was worse. Some people made jokes. This is a different kind of different, one that is not so delightful. Those who are visibly different are, in case you haven't noticed, dumber, meaner and all around less than the rest of us. We often make one of two choices: we stay away or we try to make them more like us. The first choice keeps us safer. The second choice shows how virtuous we are, for they can't rise to our level, poor things.

As if being visibly different weren't enough, illness involves us in culturally devalued experiences: quiet, solitude, introspection, withdrawal, vulnerability, failure, emptiness, intuition, emotion, ambiguity and passivity. Courage is required to overcome the subtle, but strong messages we receive that undergoing—or even *valuing*—these experiences is somehow wrong.

Here again, I find parallels between illness and creativity. The creative process invites those same experiences. Little wonder that artists have a tradition of being…untraditional. One of my sixth grade teachers was a poet and musician. He used the wall above his desk as a collage for rejection letters. One morning we came to school to find lines of his poetry (in cut-out paper letters) wrapping around the front of the building. We loved to sneak into his classroom after school to hear him wrestling Beethoven on the out-of-tune piano. He was a wonderful example of creative persistence in the face of rejection.

I remember Aesop's fable of the fox and the grapes. The fox decides, after several failed attempts to reach the grapes, that they were probably sour and not worth the effort of reaching. We teach this story to laugh at our tendency to devalue what we can't have. In the world of chronic illness, the fox may be a hero. Rather than sit beneath the grapevine wailing at his limitations, he comforts himself and moves on with his day.

Those of us who feel different (and I'll happily entertain the thought that this is everybody) can find some comfort in generating reasons why. Birth order and temperament, Myers-Briggs profile, genetic predispositions, cultural background…choose any from the menu. Once we've justified our peculiarity, the next question is: "so what?"

The disability-rights movement has given us a wonderful answer: "reasonable accommodation." The phrase refers to making changes from the norm in order to make it easier for a person with a disability to do his or her job. It is legally required of employers to make reasonable accommodations for a disabled employee. As a self-employed person, the first three reasonable accommodations I made for myself were to allow myself to walk with a cane, wear knee socks instead of pantyhose and use a "fanny pack" instead of a traditional purse. Every time I read advice about how I, as an entrepreneurial go-getter, should dress for success, I comforted myself by repeating the phrase, "reasonable accommodation."

What a wonderful world it would be if we acted as though each of us is dealing with disability and deserves reasonable accommodation. That's the reality, but it's more cost-effective if we structure our society by arranging things for the convenience of the majority and leave the minority to find ways to cope. (I have left-handed friends who are eloquent on this subject.)

Kurt Vonnegut suggested that artists are canaries. When the levels of carbon monoxide in coal mines were too high, the canaries taken there would keel over, alerting the miners to leave the mines and get to safe air. I've heard those of us dealing with autoimmune diseases put in the same role. The environment is toxic, the argument goes and those of us with some genetic predisposition are the first to fall. I am not thrilled by the idea of being an early warning system, so here's an alternate theory: Those of us who are different and who require accommodation are, in fact, encouraging the human race to evolve. Our differences may turn out to be useful or, as likely, the skill of accommodating individual needs will propel the species forward.

The moral to the story remains: Dare to be Different.

Angel Invitation Number Two: Lose Control

The elderly woman waiting for an elevator in my apartment building smiled shyly. Her blue eyes traveled from the wheels of my walker past my arms, straining to hold my body upright, to my face, scrunched with concentration and weariness. I had just walked half a block with my walker—part of a new exercise program I had set myself. "Don't worry, dear," the woman said, "it will get better." I felt a flash of heat in my chest and belly at her words. I gave her a quick smile, hoping my anger didn't show. She meant well. She believes in progress and improvement and our ability to bring them about through concerted effort. She believes in control.

One of the gifts given to me by living with an incurable chronic illness is the explosion of the myth that I am in control. When she learned I have MS, an aneurysm survivor smiled and said, "Ah, so you know you're never safe." She explained that since she was "struck down" while she was at home alone doing paperwork, she has not felt safe. Her body may, at any moment, attack her. I, too, have experienced attack where I expected none. My body is always attacking itself, destroying the fatty tissue that protects my nerves, leaving them unable to carry the messages my brain tries to send to my muscles. I am not in control of my own body.

I suspect that the idea of controlling the things around (and inside) us is a relatively new one brought about by the scientific discoveries of the past two centuries. Nineteenth century health care workers began to exert control in two areas that had heretofore eluded them: they used anesthesia to control pain and carbolic acid to control germs. Doctors could operate on their patients to fix the problems in function they discovered, courtesy of advances in the knowledge of anatomy made the century before. In this case, knowledge really was power. The more we know about how the body works (or doesn't) the more likely we can make the changes we desire.

Now we can use plastic surgery to control the appearance of our bodies. For several months, I had a plastic surgeon as a client for my Web design business. The project brought with it conflicting emotions. My Web work is always content-driven, so we were shifting the site from an initial "online brochure" with minimal information to one that educated visitors about plastic surgery. The surgeon had amassed patient questions with which to structure the site. "I want to give my daughter plastic surgery as a gift for her fourteenth birthday…" "I had a nose job one and a half years ago and a revision six months ago and still am not satisfied…" The surgeon was part of a volunteer effort that provides free reconstructive surgery to women who have facial injuries as a result of domestic abuse. In the end, my admiration for his humanitarian efforts couldn't overpower my discomfort with his cosmetic work. I referred him to another designer.

More complicated for me than when to do surgery is how to handle public health issues like diet and exercise. If eating a healthy diet can save me from developing heart disease, diabetes and a whole host of other undesirable problems (and give me more energy on a daily basis), where's the down side? Healthy eating doesn't have one. Living in fear of disease and trying to control my health through diet does. When I was on the low-fat diet and my symptoms increased, I thought, "If I weren't on this diet, it could be worse!" I had briefed my husband: if I was ever at death's door, but could still chew, he was to bring me a grilled cheese sandwich and a chocolate chip cookie. I assumed that the disease was progressing because I was not following the diet perfectly enough. For several months after I "let go" of the diet, I ate chocolate, cheese and meat with wild abandon. Then I found myself returning to more moderate and healthy, eating habits.

While I was on the diet, my cholesterol was never extremely low. Diet is only one of the factors that influence our health. We cannot escape our genetic heritage. In her book, *Women Who Run With the Wolves*, Clarissa Pinkola Estes tells a story about a friend with a gap between her two front teeth visiting the area of Africa from which her ancestors came and discovering that, not only do many women there have such a gap, it is considered a mark of beauty. Members of my husband's family are all big people. Alexis, at age four, was in the sixtieth percentile of her peers in height, the eightieth in weight. I worried, as she danced along with her "I want to be a Ballerina" video, that her heritage might deny her the dream. In case the dream and the genes both held, I was prepared with a clipping about a dance troupe called Big Dance, whose ballerinas weigh between 220 and 300 pounds.

In 1984 Jim Fixx, the author of *The Complete Book of Running* and a man credited with starting the fitness craze of the seventies, died of a heart attack while running. Fixx's father died of a heart attack at age forty-five. Fixx was fifty-two. One headline read, "Runner-author Jim Fixx couldn't outrun his genes." I agree. I also suspect that, had Fixx not run marathons and had he not ignored the chest pains that he sometimes got while running, as well as pleas from his doctor to get regular check-ups, he would have lived longer. On the other hand, we can't escape mortality.

My mother tells the story of my great Aunt Sally, who ran a nursing home in West Virginia. Upon being told by one of the aides that an elderly diabetic woman had eaten a piece of cake, she reportedly replied, "Well, hell, she might as well have it. You've gotta die of something." I find the story somewhat horrifying (maybe the horror is that my eighty-some year old mother, formerly diagnosed as "borderline diabetic," finds it funny), but Aunt Sally had a point: we are going to die.

Oregon has passed a law they call the "Death with Dignity Act" that legislates physician-assisted suicide. One doctor interviewed about it said his patients are not worried about pain, since that can be controlled with drugs. Instead, they are more worried about the loss of concentration and control over bodily functions that use of the drugs for pain-free existence engenders. They want to control the circumstances of their death and they should have that right, he believes. This is clearly a new idea. My ancestors died, willy-nilly, of such things as cancer, strokes, pneumonia and farm accidents, never for a moment suspecting control was an option.

Our quest for control extends to the other end of life as well. The most common indication for a cesarean birth is lack of progress in labor. Doctors, fearing the fetus is in distress, use a surgical procedure to remove it. One study indicated that use of a fetal monitor to reassure physicians reduces cesareans, currently at thirty percent in the U.S., by half. I was encouraged, in my childbirth classes, to develop a "labor plan," which would spell out what I wanted to have happen during the process. I made a list for the nurses of what my body would (walk with a walker) and wouldn't (walk more than fifty feet with a walker) do, but I left the planning, if any, up to the fetus. After Alexis' relatively easy delivery, my obstetrician confided that she suspects a correlation between thorough labor plans and long labors.

While I was pregnant, a relative asked me if we wanted a boy or a girl. She immediately guessed: "you don't care as long as it's healthy, right?" I looked at her from my wheelchair and said, "That wouldn't make sense, coming from me, would it?" Ralph and I declined tests which would have alerted us to various disabilities of the fetus once doctors assured us the results would not change the safety of the birth for me or the child. If the child were disabled, we would cope using the same messy and inelegant, but real life, process we've used for other challenges we've faced.

While some people may expect the alternative health care system to be less domineering, that has not been my experience. I have been a client of acupuncturists and herbalists, chiropractors and spiritual healers. After each experience, I swear never to do it again. It begins with a well-meaning sales pitch by someone who is optimistic that his or her healing work will help me. It ends with me feeling what I've nicknamed "new age guilt." If I had followed their advice more exactly, learned their techniques more thoroughly, or believed in them more completely, I would be well. New age guilt still haunts me sometimes.

For comfort, I return to what I know best: the process of creativity. I am attracted to a new painting or essay by the whisper of an idea. It is never well defined, carefully considered, or inspirationally articulated. It is a vague image, an incomplete phrase, but it carries with it a lift of the heart that tells me there is something of value in it. Creating does not come easily for me. Following the idea, I lose my way. I struggle. I swear. I sigh. I retreat. I descend into chaos. Eventually, problems are resolved or allowed, the piece is birthed and released. Knowing this about my work, I should also be able to know it about my life.

I used to attend a water exercise class for people with MS. At the same time, in other areas of the pool, toddlers were learning to swim and elderly people were swimming laps. We ended up in the locker room together. Picture it: a young mother hands the baby a cracker while she wrestles her three-year-old out of a wet, clinging, bathing suit. A huge woman with pendulous breasts helps a pale, thin elder with a bra strap. The elder helps me cajole my spasming toes into a sock. The infant watches it all from his rocking seat with serious concentration. Our bodies—thick and thin, tan and pale, flaccid and toned, small and large, continent and not, wrinkled and smooth—are wonderful. They are doing what bodies do. They are experiencing the miracle of life, which frequently propels us into unexpected, uncontrollable territory.

Angel Invitation Number Three:
Allow, Accept, Surrender

I've been asking myself about the difference between allowing and accepting. At first, I thought it was the same thing at different times. Before it happens, I allow it. After it happens, I accept it.

Allow: to let, to permit, to make provision for, to grant. Antonym: deny.

Accept: to receive, to regard as proper or true, to endure resignedly or patiently, to agree to take. Antonym: refuse, reject.

Reading those definitions, I don't want them anywhere near my disease. But I am sure they are an important part in my healing.

One discomfort I have with "allow" is that it implies that I had a choice. I think back to the philosophy that insisted that I did, in fact, choose to have MS. It's not a bad theoretical exercise. Being disabled has provided me with an easy excuse not to have a powerful career, not to accomplish too much. It has smoothed some of my rough edges; it has increased my patience and compassion. It has given me a focus for my creative output. It hasn't been all bad. The flip side of the philosophy, though, is that if I chose to be disabled, I can choose not to be. That idea has fed the monsters. If I believe that I can make myself get well, I want to try every idea I can find on a Website. I want to spend any amount of money, deny myself various pleasures, separate myself from others and despair when things do not improve. The truth is I am not in control here. I did not allow this disease.

It is helpful, though, for me to allow the disease its symptoms. If I am numb or weary or unable to move, I need to allow the sensation. Denying them, I may not do what I need to do: move or rub or rest or get help. Maybe part of the problem is language. If I say, "I am so tired and disabled that I'm going to stop moving," I will increase my fatigue and disability. On the other hand, if I deny my symptoms and keep pushing when I shouldn't or try walking without help, I'll increase my fatigue and risk injury.

The best definition of allow, in relationship to my MS, may be "make provision for". What will serve me best is to recognize my situation and make provisions for it. There's that wonderful word again: discernment.

Discernment: exhibiting keen insight and good judgment.

Once I am aware of the sensations (or lack thereof) in my body, I need to discern what action I need to take to make provision for them. There is no rule, no policy, to tell me whether I should exercise or rest. I have to pay attention and make a choice. Then I have to notice what happens, pay attention and make another choice. We are all experimenting in the laboratory of our selves.

Accepting is a happier word, for me. Someone else has dealt the cards; I am just picking them up. There's this additional piece, though, of being a good sport about it. I have to regard the situation as "right or true" and endure it patiently. Someone said the best response to the question, "Why, me?" is "Why not?" If I could wish my MS experience onto someone else, who would it be, *really*? I couldn't be that mean. Then it becomes easier to accept my MS.

Here, again, there needs to be middle ground. "She hasn't accepted reality," declared an art therapist, looking at the picture the teenaged beauty queen, now brain-injured and in a wheelchair, had drawn of herself dancing on a table. The assignment had been to "draw yourself five years from now." I wouldn't be so quick to judge (reason #439 why I am not an art therapist). I hope that girl has since danced on tables. She might have been dancing on the table right that minute: dancing out her frustration, her fears, dancing to insist on her beauty and ability. Acceptance isn't unconditional surrender.

Here, allowing and accepting look the same to me: If I reject that I have MS, I will suffer more because I won't take care of myself. If I surrender completely, I will suffer more because I will deny myself use of abilities I still have.

I am most happy and healed when I find the middle ground. The monsters insist that I must find it cautiously, consistently and perfectly. The angels agree that I may seek it joyfully, fumblingly, in syncopated time. It's the seeking, not the finding, that will polish me smooth.

Angel Invitation Number Four:
Name What's Happening

"OK, Catherine. We're all done."

I am visiting a doctor's office. It is one of the few places in my life where people call me Catherine. Instead of communicating an atmosphere of informality and comfort, the name signals me that I am in the midst of strangers.

If, when answering the phone, I hear the caller ask for "Cathy," I am thrown into confusion. Is this a long-lost friend, who knew me before I changed my name (in a rush of teenaged independence) when I was sixteen, or is it a wrong number? The pause before I answer carries thirty years of memories. Names are important.

I've been wrestling for weeks to describe the process of naming that works, for me, as an invitation to angels. In the world of Earthsea, fantasy writer Ursula K. LeGuin taught her wizards: "Magic consists in this, the true naming of a thing."

Every now and then, I realize that I have been feeling additionally tired lately, that my soul has been in shadow. My unconsidered response is to continue on, hoping the weight and darkness will lift. Sometimes they do, but often they don't. Instead, I need to discern what is happening.

First I have to be willing to seek an answer. I have to take time alone, in the quiet. I need to communicate with myself (or maybe my monsters and angels are communicating with me). I need to talk aloud or write or paint. As Captain Kirk used to say, I need to "open a channel." Then I need to have patience as emotions flare, words fail me, colors muddy. Eventually the words and emotions slow. I remember to breathe. I start recognizing this place and naming it.

Many people living with chronic illness go years without a diagnosis. Certain diseases, including MS, seem to defy definition. Symptoms come and go like the odd noise your car refuses to make when the mechanic is listening. Friends and family suspect the weakness, weariness and numbness occur too conveniently. Surely, it's all in your head. Getting a diagnosis of chronic disease, while never good news, is at least some relief. I'm not making it up; I'm not crazy; I'm not lazy; I am not alone. There is a name for this collection of physical discomforts. A correct diagnosis brings with it insight into the past, implications for the future and recommendations for action in the present. In those ways, it is a True Name.

Naming is a skill and a practice. The counselor who recommended that I wear a rubber band around my wrist was giving me practice in naming my emotions. Disregarded, they came out where they could, often zinging innocent bystanders. (It's an ongoing issue. I still imagine that Real Adults Don't Show Big Feelings and, attempting to be grown up, I try to bury my feelings under layers of stoicism.) Each time I saw the rubber band, I had to put a name to my feeling. "I was just concentrating and didn't feel anything" was not an allowable answer. Like today's preschoolers, I had to boil it down to mad, sad, glad or afraid. This relieved me of the illusion that, though I felt frustrated and annoyed, I did not feel angry. All three are variations (and, yes, I'll argue in favor of distinctions) of "mad" and it helps me to know if I spend most of my time in that territory.

Different names take me in different directions that may lead to different actions. Often, when I am sad, I pretend I am angry. If I'm irresponsibly angry, I get to rant and rave and have it be someone's fault. That is energetic fun for me. Even responsible anger takes me to enjoyable action: dancing or drawing the energy, advocating for change, inventing a new way of doing something. If I'm sad, what I need most is to cry. I don't like to cry (probably some hold over from childhood), but

I'm usually better for it. It clears my emotional being like a summer thunderstorm on the prairie clears the air. Drawing—or even ranting—in sadness doesn't work for me.

Discovering a True Name, I am left in a resourceful place. Searching for the name, I begin to discover what I want…or how I want things to change. A True Name gives me a sense not only of "what," but also of how big and for how long. I have an idea of what I can do next. Monsters sometimes suggest names that leave me squashed flat by despair. Loser. Cripple. Idiot. Monsters make moments into monuments. They make false names look true. If I am left drained, exhausted and without hope, I have not found a True Name.

Naming helps not just for the main monster, but for the attendant demons as well. My writing is one big exercise in naming. Describing my experience helps me understand it better. This may be part of the magic of "talk therapy" and support groups, where I tell my story to listening ears and open hearts. I weave a net of words around the chaos and uncertainty, limiting their movement and giving me some sense of mastery. The control is illusion and it isn't. Choosing words, I am choosing my thinking and my attitude. They are the most powerful weapons I have with which to respond to this disease.

We can help each other in naming—others certainly offer a different perspective—but we have to be careful not to impose our names on someone else's reality. From twelve-step literature: "We have not found it helpful to place labels on any degree of illness or health. We may have different symptoms, but the underlying emotions are the same or similar. We discover we are not unique in our difficulties and illnesses." There's a distinction: names and labels. A label is something slapped on the outside without understanding. A True Name emerges through intimate knowledge. If *I* try to name *your* experience, I am likely to label it. If I name *my* experience, you may gain insight into yours.

At the doctor's office, I rarely bother to correct the staff when they call me Catherine. My life is more assertive. If I call pieces of my self or my life the wrong names, my angels are quick to correct me.

"I'm just tired." No I'm not, I'm angry.

"It's just MS fatigue." Made worse by the fact that I haven't eaten in twenty hours.

"Alexis is behaving like a child." She is one. I am behaving like a child, too and I'm an adult who is feeling five years old and wants a hug.

The correction doesn't always happen that fast and that's OK too. If I insist on calling something the wrong name long enough, my sense that Something is Wrong will increase in size until it demands attention.

In the process of sifting through names, I am forced to admit I don't know The Right Answer. I have to practice accepting and entering the mystery of my life: when I look at what I think is one small facet of my life it expands until it includes the whole universe. Naming draws me into holy space and holy space into me.

I used to read descriptions of prayer and discernment and get jealous. I thought the people who practiced discernment were getting explicit instructions from God. (Maybe they are. Good for them!) Only recently have I begun to value the *practice* of discernment, the *practice* of naming. It is a microcosm of the creative process. First, I enter into the uncertainty of not knowing. Then, I have to sidestep the monsters who gather to shout their traitorous suggestions. I make a choice, being willing to be wrong. I take action and wait for correction or relief. Instead of God sending an answer, God is asking questions. Explicit instructions would make me more confident; Naming increases my compassion.

While naming helps me separate myself from the disease, it also pulls me into relationship with it. To name it, I must pay attention to it and

my experience of it. I watch as its strength or importance grows or shrinks, as sensations move from here to there, as its expression becomes harder or softer. Naming allows my monster to be Other, but it also claims it as mine, to know and to accompany, to have and to hold. We will dance together until death do us part.

Angel Invitation Number Five: Trust

Luckily for me, perfection is not required for creativity or dealing with chronic illness or life in general. I am spectacularly bad at trusting God, but it turns out that's OK.

One of the twelve steps—and part of many other spiritual practices—is to surrender one's life to a higher power. With my usual tendency to black-and-white thinking, I imagined this was a one-time thing. Put God in the driver's seat and let go of the steering wheel. Once and for all. World without End. Amen. I struggled mightily with whether I could take this step. What if God wanted something horribly inconvenient of me? If I turned my life over to God, was the next step a plane ticket to Africa to become a missionary? What would my husband do? I hesitated and worried. Members of my EA support group came to my aid by describing their real-life process…the same one I find myself living now.

Do I trust God? Yes and yes and yes. There are certain things I need to believe about God in order to practice that trust.

God is good. For the first fifteen years of my life, I affirmed this at every meal. In the fourteenth century, a Christian mystic called Julian of Norwich had a series of visions she spent the rest of her life understanding. She worried about people who (biographer James Kiefer writes) "through no fault of their own had never heard the Gospel. She never received a direct answer to her questions about them, except to be told that whatever God does is done in Love and therefore 'that all shall be well and all shall be well and all manner of thing shall be well.' " God, Julian understood, is all about love.

I heard Rabbi Harold Kushner talk about Hurricane Katrina. He was firm in his belief that Katrina was not a judgment of God upon the people of the Gulf Coast. "God was not in the storm," he said, quoting from scripture. "God was in the reaction of people to the storm...the outpouring of compassion, of generosity..."

A good, loving God would not give me MS, either as a punishment or a teaching tool. Because of God's grace, I am able to find the gifts hidden in the experience of illness. Through God's mercy, my struggles have brought me in God's direction. Among God's people, I am valued, cared for, challenged and comforted. Because God is love, I can trust.

God is Mystery. Imagine, psychologist Dan Johnston suggests, you are a two-dimensional being in a two-dimensional world. You understand height and width. You visit a three-dimensional world and find out about depth. Then you return home and try to describe what you saw. How can you do it? That is what Jesus is trying to do when he says the Kingdom of God is like...a mustard seed that grows...yeast that spreads...a treasure hidden in a field. He's trying to explain the third dimension to a two-dimensional world. It's impossible, but he wants us to understand that there is More.

I find myself impatient with people who conceive of God as a short-order cook. "We needed a refrigerator with a door that hinged on the right. We looked and couldn't find one. We prayed about it and there was an ad in the paper the next day." The God of my understanding does not micromanage the universe. If God's gonna give you a refrigerator door, what about making me walk? What about imposing world peace?

Sometimes people do find a refrigerator door; sometimes those who were lame begin to walk; sometimes there is an outbreak of peace. I don't understand why it happens and why it doesn't. I don't believe (contrary, I realize, to some Biblical testimony) that God plays favorites. I am confident that God is bigger and better than I have any hope of understanding. Happily, my understanding is not required for the universe to continue to function. Because God is mystery, I can trust.

God is miraculous. As I was growing up, I had a Corita Kent poster on my wall that said, "To believe in God is to believe that all the rules will be fair and that there will be wonderful surprises." I was home from college, buzzing from the effects of the intravenous steroids given me to combat my first MS exacerbation. The diagnosis was less than a week old. My mother saw the poster as she was tucking me into bed. "Do you still believe that?" she asked. "Yes," I answered without thinking. I have thought about it since and I still believe it.

At the moment, MS in incurable and my MS is progressive. Still, I can surrender to my higher power; I can trust in God. Because God is good, I will not listen to demons who speak of guilt and punishment. I will find rest in understanding that, regardless of my circumstances or the state of my health, all is well. Because God is beyond my understanding, I will not torture myself with questions of why or what if. I will make choices and take action that support health. Because God is miraculous, I will be on the lookout for wonderful surprises.

Getting to a New Normal

My body goes into a bit of a decline. It doesn't feel like "a bit," of course, not to my dramatic monster-mind. It feels, rather, like the Beginning of the End. I label it as such when it starts on my birthday. When I move out of my monster-mind, I realize that I have lost a small but important function. Years ago, I lost the ability to put my weight on my right leg. (It collapses at the knee joint when I try.) I've compensated by using my left leg for independent stand-pivot transfers. Now my left leg is failing me. With that loss I enter a time of Big Emotions (fear, anger, grief) and frustrating experimentation. At some point, this transition time will calm and there will be a New Normal. I just have to get there.

It had been a busy week. Ralph was out of town on a business trip. On Monday, my brothers and their wives visited and took Alexis and me to dinner before we went to her swimming class. Tuesday, two of Alexis' friends (nine and ten year old neighbors) joined us for the evening. The girls made dinner: Banquet fried chicken and tater tots alongside fresh peas and apples. Wednesday, I had my annual review at work and then the girls came with us to McDonalds and puppet practice at church. I was aware of being increasingly tired and missed the transfer between the driver's seat and scooter when we got to church. Ministerial staff got me back up and functioning so I could (a) go to Bible study while the girls joined other puppeteers and (b) give the girls a ride home (transferring the other direction with no problem.)

Ralph got in at about eleven that night, a bit earlier than expected due to tailwinds.

Thursday after work I visited a church member who was dealing with cancer. Then I came home, helped Alexis with homework and headed to church again for a committee meeting.

By the time I got home, I could feel a migraine coming on and took a pill for it, wondering as I did if I'd ever taken migraine medicine on the same night as my Avonex (interferon for MS) injection. Possibly not. The next day, I needed Ralph's help to transfer to the shower stool and again to the driver's seat. That's not unheard of on a "shot day," and I assumed that I would gain some strength before getting to work. Arriving there, I could tell that wasn't the case and flagged down a passing painter to lift me from the driver's seat into the scooter. (Like Blanche DuBois, I have always depended on the kindness of strangers.) A couple hours later, a coworker helped me in the bathroom. (I could manage the transfers, but couldn't stand long enough to pull up my underwear.) Many people were leaving early, fleeing the paint fumes. One coworker helped me transfer to the driver's seat, another offered to follow me home and help me there. Arriving home, we missed the transfer and I ended up on the van floor. I can't use my legs to get up, so we called 911. Fifteen minutes later the EMTs showed up and lifted me onto the scooter. They saw me safely inside. An hour or so later, I managed a bathroom transfer on my own. Alexis came home and, later, Ralph, bringing take-out Indian for my birthday dinner. We went to bed early.

In the four months since then, I have fallen once or twice a week, attempting to transfer between the scooter and the driver's seat, the toilet, or the bed. If I fall in the van, I have to call 911. (Cue anger, embarrassment and shame.) Like the construction sites boasting "57 days with no work accidents," I move into each day counting: "14 days since my last 911 call."

The most spectacular fall was back against the toilet. The toilet tank broke and I sat there while a waterfall rushed around me. It was evening; the rental townhouse maintenance workers had gone home. We turned off the water to the toilet, called the emergency number, left a message explaining the situation and waited. A couple hours later a maintenance worker arrived with a plunger. We showed him the toilet and he went away. The next morning he came back with a toilet. The new toilet is slightly lower and longer than the old one, just enough difference that I've been having trouble standing up from it, even with grab bars.

I had my annual neurology visit shortly after the decline began and described my distress. As a result, we've added a medication meant to prevent migraines. (Two months along we have one miss and one hit on my monthly three-day agonies.) I've visited a physical therapist several times and have begun to use a transfer board in the car. An occupational therapist will soon visit me at work to strategize safer bathroom transfers there. Meanwhile, I have begun to gather information on next steps: personal care attendants, chore services, adult day care. The nerve connection that enabled me to stand on my left leg for long enough to move from one seat to another (and to arrange my underwear and skirts before sitting) was powering my independence. Now that it is failing, I am rethinking the way I dress, drive, work, relax and…excrete. Six months from now I will either do things differently or I will not do them at all. (Nudity would solve many problems, but I live in the wrong culture and climate!) In the meantime, I am in the muck of transition.

I want, through sheer willpower, to do things the Old Way and have it work. Surely, this is just a blip on the health radar that will disappear! Maybe if I exercised more, I would gain strength?

"It's not about your muscles," says the physical therapist. "The nerves' messages aren't there anymore."

I am angry at my body, angry at the health care system and angry at a punishing God in whom I don't even believe! (My God is a loving one but, at times like this, a more primitive, vengeful stand-in appears.)

Luckily, an angel has also appeared, in the form of a disability veteran, a woman who survived polio fifty-four years ago. "When I get into anger I have to get out of it," she advised me, "and the best way is through positive action." She is a woman of her word, advocating from her wheelchair against poverty and in favor of the environment and

144

historical preservation. I almost jumped up to go to a meeting as soon as I read her email. Action, yeah, let's go!

Twenty-five years ago, I remember a career counselor saying to me, "The word I keep hearing from you is useful. You want to be useful." And the word my monster stabs at me is "useless." Can't drive? Can't work? Can't go to the bathroom without help? Useless! Useless! Useless! Allowances I might make for others do not, somehow, apply to me.

My memory unearths a story from my college Chinese Philosophy class.

"This tree is useless!" Hui Tzu snorted.
"Trunk all swelled up curved.
Branches all gnarled up crooked.
A carpenter would toss away his tools
And bust out laughing.
A builder wouldn't give it a second glance.
This is one useless snarl of wood.
Your ideas are like that, too:
Strong enough, but tough to use."

Chuang Tzu said, "Usefulness is tricky.
The wildcat and weasel think they're great hunters.
They leap around any old how and get caught in a net or trap.
The yak is so huge it almost blocks out the sun,
But it's no good for catching mice.
This big old tree of yours…
Wander around beside it!
Take a nap beneath it!
No one's gonna chop it down.
No one's gonna carve it up.
No one's gonna hurt it.
What is there about its uselessness
That gets you so riled up?"

Usefulness is tricky. Of course I'd rather become part of a stately mansion than offer somebody shade! I want to be part of the hustle and bustle, not stand out here in this empty field! But if I lift my head up out of the pity pot, I see things I can do. I can listen. I can watch. I can be honest. I can encourage.

I am moving to a new normal. It's not easy. It's not graceful. But it is possible.

Note for the second edition:

I have been through several "new normals" since this manuscript first went to press. I can no longer transfer from my wheelchair, even with a transfer board. Within the last year, I have had surgeries to install a baclofen pump (for spasticity) and a suprapubic catheter and to treat a decubitus ulcer. I have been approved for personal care attendant services, which takes some of the load off Ralph. I am learning about how to live in a wheelchair, both in terms of physical care and new, yet familiar, ways to dance with my monster mind. I return to the principles in this book, reminding myself to be patient and merciful during times of overwhelm and incubation, search diligently for what matters during reconciliation and embrace rededication with joy. Always, my life is better if I let the creative process be my teacher.

Do-be-do-be-do: Things to Do While You're Healing

When I began to consider healing as a chronic and creative process, I came up with a list of "healing tasks" to move things along. Five years later, I decided the list was hopelessly prescriptive, an exercise in control, a sign of youthful pride. Ten years later, I'm realizing that these activities are a natural part of my process. They probably aren't necessary, but they're helpful and, in the spirit of full disclosure, I'll include them.

I am an off-and-on student of meditation. (This is exactly how you're *not* supposed to do it.) Every few years, I get a "dose" of meditation instruction and return to regular practice. Like many things in my life, my meditation practice ebbs and flows. Meditation is paying attention to mind and body and anchoring myself in the present moment. As I sit, thoughts, images and sensations arise and dissolve. In my early days, I thought my mind was hopelessly more active than anyone else's and I despaired of ever "getting it right." I thought that, with enough practice, I would be able to "just be." (A voice—demonic or angelic?—suggests that I have never practiced enough.) What has happened is an increase in compassion for myself, an ability to appreciate the planning-worrying-dreaming-listing-controlling spirals of my mind for the comedy that they are. I pictured "releasing attachments" a quiet activity, like a butterfly release. Instead, it's a vaudeville show. Even with my lamentable practice patterns, meditation has become part of my life; notice how often I use the word "breathe."

Through meditation we learn about our attachments and practice releasing them. Releasing our attachments to feeling a certain way (physically and emotionally), to our reputations, to taking action, we release our selves. We make room for the present moment. The process of practicing meditation involves opening out, attending and accepting. In many ways, healing is a meditation practice.

Visualization, creating and manipulating mental pictures, is a bit different. Many people advocate it for those of us with chronic illness. I believe that there is a danger in approaching visualization with a heroic attitude: we visualize our cancer cells disappearing and then become grief-stricken and guilt-ridden when medical tests do not reflect our practice. Still, visualization can open us to our own inner images, to our subconscious, to the richness of our minds. For instance, we can visualize how our symptoms look in our body and imagine them telling us something of importance. We can visualize a healing place and sink into the bliss of being there, even if we can't physically leave our hospital bed. We can heal old hurts by holding conversations in our imagination with people or events long past. Allowing the images that arise and accepting them, *playing* with them, we open ourselves to healing possibilities.

Some method of paying attention directly to the sensations arising from our bodies can be helpful. When we experience illness, we often feel that our bodies have betrayed us. We detach our "selves" from our bodies, making our physical being an "other." Our rage becomes directed toward it, as mine does when I hit my legs in frustration. Practicing self-massage and body therapy helped me reconnect with my body at a deeper level. I developed compassion for it and felt a life-long separation from my body begin to heal. It was in thinking about my relationship with my body that I chose the word "reconciliation" to name one period of the chronic healing process. While meditation includes body awareness, there are other practices, such as t'ai chi, yoga and massage, which more specifically focus on the body. Body awareness techniques can bring us back into our bodies, an essential part of returning to wholeness.

There are few culturally-endorsed activities to mark our passages in the healing process. We receive get well cards, encouraging us to move quickly to a happy ending. We receive visitors, before whom we often feel obligated to appear strong, hopeful and cheerful. After the cards are opened and the well-wishers have gone home (or even stopped visiting), we are left in the murk of the healing process, with nothing to light our way. For centuries, human beings have used rituals as ways to recognize and support transforming life events. On the tenth anniversary of my MS diagnosis, Ralph and I sat near small piles of roses and pine boughs. We told each other the story of the days leading to the diagnosis. We took turns putting a rose into the vase in front of us, naming a gift the MS had brought into our lives and then putting a pine bough into the vase, naming a difficulty the disease had brought us. Such rituals serve to acknowledge the transformations we undergo as we move through the periods of our healing process.

Part of discovering and accepting who we are involves releasing who we feel we should be, but are not. Reviewing our personal history and acknowledging the messages we received from our family and culture brings them to consciousness and allows us to make choices about what to accept or move beyond. My journey has included explorations of myself as woman, youngest child, cripple, mystic and artist in a culture that devalues those roles. Reviewing the messages I have received about who I am has given me strength to express these unfashionable identities. Peeling back the layers of expectations that have encircled our lives gives us room to express our essence.

Creative expression can lead us to what gives us joy. Rediscovering joy is an important part of the period of rededication. Playing with art materials in an open and accepting environment can bring us to a connection with other creative and expressive parts of ourselves. In an experiment conducted at the University of Montreal, participants created fifteen "mess paintings" each day for six weeks. To make a mess painting, participants opened sheets of newspaper and painted on them with eight colors of poster paints, trying to make the biggest mess they could in two minutes. After six weeks of practicing mess painting, participants reported that they were able to deal more successfully with problems, had more realistic and positive self-concepts, felt more self-confident, felt more interested in the arts and nature, and had taken new interest in formerly abandoned hobbies (some of which did not fit any stereotype of "creative activity"). Pure creative expression had led them to connect with their own passions. Six weeks of mess painting (on my own—forget the "open and accepting environment") marked a return to art making that continues to this day.

Some form of each of these activities—meditation, body awareness, ritual making, exploring cultural messages and creative expression—have become part of my dance. If I look at each as a practice, I am gentle with myself. I paint, for instance, not to produce a painting, not to increase my skill at painting, not to make extra money, but because painting allows me to practice the creative process. Painting, I am facing the emptiness of the blank space. I am gathering the courage to make a mark. I am valuing my own vision. I am making mistakes and integrating them. I am stumbling upon limitations and coping with them. I am encountering surprises and celebrating them. I am finding completion and resting in it. Practicing painting I am practicing healing and practicing living. It is not about accomplishment. It is, however, a way to trick that part of me that craves accomplishment. While "don't just do something, sit there!" is a great slogan for those who meditate, telling myself I'm "doing meditation" is easier for my over-active personality than saying "I'm just being."

These are the ways I practice healing. I am called to these movements as music calls us to the next move in a dance.

Creative Experiments in Rededication

Rules Review:

1. Use the materials and spaces of your choice: fancy or plain, special or ordinary, comfortable or challenging. It may help to pretend you're a little kid.

2. Do what you like (or change it so you *do* like it) and leave the rest.

3. Just once, try doing the one that seems most outside your comfort zone.

4. Be gentle with yourself.

5. Have fun.

Writing Starters:

Write the starter words and then keep going, keeping the words coming one after another even if you're writing "I don't know what to say next, but if I did...".

- My favorite way to ward off monsters is...

- My favorite way to invite angels is...

- The surroundings I find most healing are...

- If I were eccentric, I would...

- If I gave up control...

- I want to accept...

- What's happening is...

- I wish I had a ceremony to recognize...

- When I pay attention, I notice…
- Recently, I've learned…
- Healing, for me, is…
- Once upon a time…

Making your Mark:

With the mark-making utensils of your choice (color adds meaning and fun), make marks in response to the suggestion. Be as sketchy—or as elaborate—as you want to be.

- Make protective marks.
- Make inviting marks.
- Make meditative marks.
- Make a mess.

Objects in Space:

Find a flat surface you can use for these experiments. You need to be able to leave it, have it be undisturbed, and come back to it the next day. Find household or run-of-the-mill objects or make your own.

- Choose an object to represent yourself and other objects to represent monsters and/or angels. Position these objects so that you are protected from the monsters but vulnerable to angels. What arrangements or additional objects will make this possible? Come back in a day or two and look at the space. Do you have what you need? How might things change?

Sounding it Out:

Start with a rhythm—clap or tap on a surface. Add a repetitive sound—pitch, volume and duration are up to you. If you're a musician, feel free to use an instrument. If you're "not a musician," use your voice and body to make noise. Break free of the repetition and experiment.

- Sound like protection.

- Sound like openness.

- Sound surprising.

- Sound like chaos.

- Sound like calm.

- Sound like celebration.

So the Drama:

Set up two empty chairs, facing each other. As you change roles, move from one chair to the other. Feel free to get up and move around. If someone unexpected shows up, add a chair.

- One of your monsters and one of your angels tell each other their true names and then plan a party together.

Move Through it:

Make your body into a pose representing the idea: adjust your facial expression, how you hold your head and torso, how you position your arms and legs. Once you have the pose, begin to move out of it. Let how fast you move, how you move and how you're using the space grow from the idea.

- You discover each part of your body anew and recognize and celebrate its wholeness.

Shall We Dance?

Something has changed. Our bodies or minds are thrown into disorganization. We experience racing and confused thoughts, physical pain and weariness. Our focus narrows until we experience only our suffering. Demons rush in to declare the endlessness of our losses, the burdensomeness of our needs, our worthlessness to the universe. We are completely overwhelmed.

We have no choice but to give in. We rest, sleep, cease to struggle, crave quiet. We lapse into a formless state of passivity—an incubation period.

Our emergence from incubation is marked by our recognition of moments of release from suffering. Angels begin to flock around us. We understand, in these numinous moments of grace, that, in this instant, nothing need change. We begin to experience and accept our true selves. We form new relationships with our bodies, minds and souls.

Having connected with our souls, we are called to express our essential being. We release ourselves (at least in part) from cultural and familial expectations. We rededicate ourselves to doing what gives us joy.

This process is a healing dance. It doubles back on itself, skips and jumps. It balances between doing and being, between movement and stillness.

I have said enough, for now, about my dance. I'm sitting here smiling at the ridiculousness of it. I'm breathless at my own audacity.

Transform the rhythms of everyday struggle into a creative project? Ennoble my nasty, negative "self-talk" by imagining it a gaggle of demons pushing me toward healing? Assert that my weaknesses stand shoulder to shoulder with the values Mama taught me to create a band of angels? And then top it all by imagining this is some sort of journey into God?!? Harumpf.

But you know what? Understanding it that way has kept me going, kept me painting and writing, working and worshipping, for more than twenty-five years. Wrestling with these ideas moves me from depression to trust, from desolation to surrender, from stubbornness to choice, from ambition to faith. I am crabby and whiny, ill and exhausted AND I am blessed, blessed, blessed.

By considering the ways in which the healing process is a creative one, we can enlarge our vision of healing to include what is usually called "illness." We can recognize the whole process and increase our compassion for those who suffer. Disability and death are no longer seen as failures, but become parts of the process. By understanding that this process is constantly active in all of us (and we in it), we cease to distance ourselves from our experience and from each other. Reconnecting with ourselves and with each other, we find God.

Here we are, monsters and angels and I, dancing in hazardous terrain. My dance may not be graceful or polished, but, with it, I move toward God instead of running away. When the music starts and the monsters and angels grab you by the hands, your dance may look nothing like mine. I hope, as you discover your dance, that you will tell me—and others—about it. It's not as fun to dance alone.

Shall we dance?

155

Becoming

You stand there
sheepish
bewildered
pieces of your life
strewn all around you.

What happened?
Bits you swore
were part of you
have crawled away
across the floor
are hiding in dark corners
refusing to come to you.
Scraps you never
thought to claim
are jumping against your legs
begging to be picked up.
What to make of it?

Give in.
Whine and bitch and moan
if you like.
Say that life is unfair,
that this isn't what they promised.
Swear revenge.

Give in.
Laugh and chortle and giggle
when you're ready.
Sing a song.
Dance a jig.
Celebrate the paradox.

Then gather up the
colors at your feet
the browns and grays and blues
the yellows the reds the greens
Hug them close.
Treasure them.
Make yourself a cloak.

www.ingramcontent.com/pod-product-compliance
Lightning Source LLC
Chambersburg PA
CBHW070833310526
45788CB00017B/556

* 9 7 8 1 4 5 3 6 8 6 3 3 1 *